Acts of Revision

A GUIDE FOR WRITERS

Edited by

Wendy Bishop

Boynton/Cook
HEINEMANN
Portsmouth, NH

Boynton/Cook Publishers, Inc.
A subsidiary of Reed Elsevier Inc.
361 Hanover Street
Portsmouth, NH 03801–3912
www.boyntoncook.com

Offices and agents throughout the world

The authors and pubisher wish to thank those who have generously given permission to reprint borrowed material:

Portions of *Revision Revisited* by Alice S. Horning. Published by Hampton Press, 2002. Used by permission of the publisher.

Library of Congress Cataloging-in-Publication Data
Acts of revision : a guide for writers / edited by Wendy Bishop.
    p. cm.
   Includes bibliographical references.
    ISBN 0-86709-550-4 (alk. paper)
    1. Editing. I. Bishop, Wendy. II. Title.
   PN162.A24 2004
   808'.042—dc22   2003022994

Editor: Lisa Luedeke
Production editor: Sonja S. Chapman
Cover design: Jenny Jensen Greenleaf
Compositor: Tom Allen
Manufacturing: Steve Bernier

Printed in the United States of America on acid-free paper
08   07   06   05   04   VP   1   2   3   4   5

Contents

Introduction

Eat Like an Owl!

Writers consume more than they produce. Their meals include words, images, landscapes, memories, books, thoughts, emotions, and hours, among other things. They are omnivorous in their search for sustenance, for ideas and images. Taking in more than they need, authors boil down, forge, simmer, concoct, fabricate, assemble, *rethink,* and *revise.* Their processes can take hours—even days, weeks, lifetimes! It is no small task to turn raw input (drafts) into polished output (a public product). You're free to indulge when you write, without guilt, because having more pages available to revise assures that you have more options open to you as you shape your draft to meet your aims. "Eat like an owl," Peter Elbow tells writers, "take in everything and trust your innards to digest what's useful and discard what's not."

This collection assumes you're ready to eat like an owl, and it will help you develop trust in your own work by offering you insights into revision processes. You don't have to twist writers' arms very hard to learn that they have philosophies of revision. Abstract these authors' beliefs from the short quotes shared here:

> I read once that some people start off by writing sentence by sentence or word by word and they never go back and revise. They just write headlong into it. Or some people always know the ending before they begin. It works in different ways for different people. When these stories started off they were really rough, but they changed and it wasn't just mindless or effortless. It was work. —Amy Tan

> Everything should be made as simple as possible, but not simpler. —Albert Einstein

> It is no less difficult to write a sentence in a recipe than sentences in *Moby Dick.* So you might as well write *Moby Dick.* —Annie Dillard

> Paul Valery speaks of the "une ligne donné" of a poem. One line is given to the poet by God or by nature, the rest he has to discover for himself. —Stephen Spender

> I researched the OED [Oxford English Dictionary] to find out how the word *hangnail* developed, how it gets used in idioms, and how its meaning changed over time. I searched beauty books for information on what causes hangnails

and how to take care of them. I researched newspapers to find out if hang-
nails had shown up in recent news (they had, and both instances ended up in
the essay). —Kristina Emick

I am so composed that nothing is real unless I write it. —Virginia Woolf

Just as you study the habits and practices of other writers (and read their
writing with your writing in mind), you'll benefit from considering how you
feel about and have learned to revise. For instance, today as you read this
book, what sort of reviser are you? (*Hint:* If you don't know what identities
are available for you to choose from, consult Chapters 1, 3, and 4 as soon as
you can.) Are you a single drafter—a writer who sits down and writes a pretty
coherent first draft that needs little improvement before submission—or do you
often need to rework initial rough drafts, like Amy Tan? Do you learn what you
want to say as you write, what you think about your life, in the manner of
Virginia Woolf? Or do you initially assemble voices and information that other
sources provide in a manner similar to that described by Kristina Emick? Are
you a pragmatist like Annie Dillard (just write, worry later) or a romantic (listen to your inspiration and it will guide you) or somewhere in between, like
Paul Valery, who realizes we are given writing gifts but we also earn our pages
through hard work?

The authors who contributed to this collection understand that revising
matters, but they also realize it's an aspect of the composing process that is
difficult to study. Our chapters are designed to invite you into the acts of revision that we know are productive. We share hints. Offer insights. Help you consider your options. Share our experiences, including what doesn't work and
why.

In general, authors in this collection will be considering revision as the
practice of making meaningful changes in texts at the word, sentence, paragraph, and full text level by adding, deleting, substituting, and rethinking
their work entirely. As editors, they are concerned with assuring the text has
consistency and, at times, that is conforms to "house style": the requirements
of a class or publisher. As proofreaders, they check to make sure their revisions and their editing has been completed carefully and that no typographical errors mar their best presentation of their texts and thinking. Obviously,
these terms can and should be defined by all writers for the contexts in which
they are working.

Revision takes you from self to society, from the writer's concerns to the
readers' concerns. When you write in a journal, as many of us do, outsiders
don't matter. This is safe space where we can be corny, take risks, trail off
vaguely into interesting side streets. We learn a great deal from this sort of writing, but we do so in a less systematic way than when we revise. To revise, writers must compare versions, consider alternate methods of development and
organization, assess the quality of their communication, and play, often with
style options.

Obviously, to compare and contrast, to control and to play, to assess and to experiment requires time and forbearance. Writers and those who work with writers need to learn from play and risk by studying mistakes in order to incorporate new skills. They need to be able to make and take chances in their writing in order to see how the options stack up against each other.

At times, it helps to freeze-frame revision moves, thinking about the demands of an early draft or the demands of a near-final draft, or to focus on general strategies and then genre strategies—the demands of pleasing readers of poetry compared with the demands of readers of private essays and business memos. Writers who enjoy revising are often those who enjoy looking at convention and experimentation in tandem, as equal partners in the composing process.

If you're a rebel at heart and don't like anyone telling you how to write, that's fine. You can still learn a lot and mush around on your own. Or you can try again, new, with each draft, or not revise at all. However, if you adopt this last stance, you risk not being read. Agatha Christie expresses the problem more elegantly: "If you like to write for yourself only, that is a different matter—you can make it any length, and write it in any way you wish; but then you will probably have to be content with the pleasure alone of having written it." In fact, you need others to revise wisely. You need to share your work with supportive readers (peers, friends, family) on the road to learning to share with more demanding critics. You need to learn to forgive yourself and play and to become your own most demanding reader; that is, you need to know which role is most appropriate for which moment. Many writers forgo the pleasures of writing for others because they are thin-skinned. Often, they fail to understand that response to their writing is just that: response. Like an owl, they can eat what they want, use what they need, and discard the rest. Owls do this naturally; writers learn from practice.

In *Acts of Revision: A Guide for Writers*, authors seek to help you consider and overcome any resistance you may feel toward revising. In the opening chapter, Brock Dethier encourages you to tune up your attitude toward the art of reseeing your work. In Chapter 2, I urge you to increase the depth of your text before you start to remove material from your word-hoard; all writers don't do this with every project, but they do all know how this process works. While I'm clearly from the "eat all you can" smorgasbord school of revising, Hans Ostrom, in Chapter 3, believes you can learn from changing the *masks* you use as you approach your work. Working from a stockpile of research into expert writers' revision processes, Alice Horning, in Chapter 4, offers fourteen ways to practice the art of revision based on this data.

Continuing the conversation begun in Chapter 2, in Chapter 5, Melissa Goldthwaite discusses why you need to be your own audience and how you can take risks in your writing but also study the results of such behaviors. In her chapter, you'll discover that rule breaking is not a sin in the land of revision. In fact, it's useful. For pleasure in language choice for the writer translates into reading pleasure for an audience. In Chapter 6, Maggie Gerrity reviews her personal revision history as an author in several genres.

The authors of Chapter 7 and Chapter 8 move the collection focus from revising in general to revising at the level of style, to improve the sound and effect of your text, particularly your sentences. I admit that I can't inoculate you with "sentence sense" in Chapter 7; instead, I provide a range of exercises that allow you to imitate published and peer writers and to learn something about sentence patterns. In Chapter 8, Devan Cook renews your acquaintance with punctuation but not in a prescriptive way. She examines the ways punctuation choice alters and signals your meaning. Study with her, and you'll learn to use punctuation for your own best purposes.

The final chapters, 9 through 12, take up revising issues that are of interest to authors of creative nonfiction and poetry and hypertext. Chapter 9 finds me reviewing definitions of creative nonfiction and the revision-complicating issues of fact and fiction and memory and truth. Advice for revising with these concerns in mind are offered in the chapter exercises. Laura Newton tackles the subject of revision in poetry in Chapter 10. Some, often novice, poets believe authors in this genre are "born not made," but Chapter 10 suggests the reverse is more likely. Via revision, poets have a hand in their own nativity. Dana Kantrowitz, in Chapter 11, turns her poetic process inside out, letting you sit with her as she composes a new poem. As you read about revising poetry, remember that many of the exercises and much of the advice from these (and other) chapters can be adapted to other genres. In the final chapter, Jay Szczepanski considers composing and revising multimedia. While most of the authors in this collection focus on revision of print texts, similar *and* unexpected revision challenges await those who will continue to revise their lives and their texts during the twenty-first century.

In fact, authors in *Acts of Revision: A Guide for Writers* aim to complicate the image of the writer who writes alone. We do so because it just isn't true. Writers compose and revise in any number of social and collaborative contexts. To illustrate this, included as afterwords is an interview that my regular coauthor, Hans Ostrom, and I conducted on email. After reading our collaborative revision history, you'll find yourself remembering moments when other chapter authors focused your attention on the interactive nature of revising.

Discussions and exercises in this collection suggest that you should share with readers and work to incorporate readers' and writers' practices into your repertoire. Revision isn't just for school writers or for creative writers, and collaborative revision takes place in many, if not most, business and technical settings, as scientists prepare a research report, lawyers a brief, a government unit a review. The more you know about yourself as a reviser, the effect of revision on your writing, and the options that are available, the more you'll be able to participate in a number of these writing worlds. Teacher Lil Brannon explains her pleasure in collaborative revision this way:

That's why I write a lot with other people. That and it's never quite as lonely. That and it's just plain more fun. You get to talk a lot. You get to hear yourself think. The best collaborations I've had were those where there was a lot of talk, where we would talk out the ideas and write as we talked, dictate the piece. The first draft would be a conglomerate of stuff—talked-out ideas, sixteen examples, a ramble or two here and there. A draft much like my [own] first drafts—way too long, a few gems hidden within a jungle. Then, each of us would try our hand at making it right—working on this part here, that part there, adding and deleting, whatever it needed. Then we would meet and see what we had and cut and write and add and subtract together. . . . The writing never seemed hard either—time consuming but not hard.

Place yourself in a similar state of talk and play; revise alone, revise with others.

We hope you'll read our chapters as you work on your writing. If you've always wanted a short course in this particular aspect of composing, here it is. If you're using the book with a writing group, you might preface a draft-sharing session with a discussion of a chapter you have agreed to read beforehand. This way, you may be able to compound your insights. If you're using this book in a writing classroom, your teacher may assign the entire class to read chapters as you undertake course units or paper sequences. She may ask you to focus on particular chapters or even exercises within chapters as you work on the draft of your paper.

You'll certainly find it useful to bring the book with you to one-to-one conferences with your teacher or to the writing center tutor you work with. Your need for advice will certainly vary. Right now you may not need to revise poems but maybe you really could use help understanding how punctuation can change your essay.

This book may be your only outside reading in a course focused on drafting and revising your own and classmates' work. Or it may join other texts—readings by other writers that you can use for some of the suggested imitations or a handbook of rules that you can put in dialogue with some of the reasoned rule breaking suggested in particular chapters here.

Try to undertake at least some of these revision explorations in judgment- and grade-free zones. You need to take risks and learn from mistakes in order to strengthen your overall writing. Consider teacher Mimi Schwartz's characterization:

> To value self-investment, to avoid premature closure, to see revision as discovery, to go beyond the predictable, to risk experimentation, and, above all, to trust your own creative powers are necessary for all good writing, whether it is a freshman theme, a poem, a term paper. . . . Few of us reward risk taking that fails with a better grade than polished but pedestrian texts. We

are more product-oriented, judging assignments as independent of one another rather than as part of a collective and ongoing body of work. No wonder that students interpret our message as "Be careful, not creative!"

The authors in this collection join me in encouraging you to be creative as well as to be careful when you cast and recast your words for interested readers.

Acknowledgments

To Lisa Luedeke and the always helpful staff at Boynton/Cook, thanks for teaching me the pleasures of collaboration. I'm in debt to Hans Ostrom for bucketfuls of writing enthusiasm. Student writing anchors this collection. Thanks in particular to those in recent years who have followed me on a brisk study of revision and style. We've practiced and played—in the classroom, online, and in community writing groups. None of you has ever undertaken revision that I haven't found instructive. And, as always, thank you for trusting me to share your work.

My family has branched and blended, and grown; they've taught me that it's truly impossible to draft too much, for each new version reveals new richness.

For Dean, who believes every day that flat Gulf swells will alter into surf. One storm not so long ago, he was right. He has taught me to believe and to play and to eat like an owl.

Tallahassee, Fall 2003

One

Revising Attitudes

Brock Dethier

In writing and revision, attitude is everything. If you have a bad attitude toward writing, you might be able to do well on standardized tests by identifying parts of speech and completing vocabulary analogies, but your writing probably isn't as good as it could be. You turn in first drafts as soon as you can bullshit your way to the page minimum or to the point where you figure your boss will stop reading and skip to the summary. You view revision as a bad joke that English teachers dreamt up to prolong the torture of homework.

You aren't the only one who resists revision. Every professional writer knows the sinking feeling of reading the editor's critique and thinking, "I have to do that *again*?!" My own writing group has nurtured most of the writing I've done during the past six years, yet every time I take something to the group, I relearn how resistance to revision feels; I revisit the feeling that I don't have the energy to do what my colleagues want me to do. So my concern in this chapter is not "How can I get novice writers to see the obvious value of revision?" but "What do all writers need to see, think, and do to improve our attitudes toward revision?"

Before you conclude that you fit the bad-attitude stereotype I've sketched here, let me make clear: You already are a reviser. You already like revisions. You revise every time you hit the delete key, every time you insert. You revise phrases in your head before you even start typing. Everything you read has been revised, and everything you listen to. It's a rare CD that doesn't contain at least one revision of another performer's work, whether it's Tori Amos' reworking of Nirvana's "Smells Like Teen Spirit" or Run-DMC's version of Aerosmith's "Walk This Way." Revision is everywhere. If you're going to write for the rest of your life—and most adults do—the question is not whether you will embrace revision, but when.

Improving your attitude toward revision can revolutionize your writing and your enjoyment of it. With a positive attitude toward revision, you will listen to feedback with an open ear and not get so quickly offended when a reader tries to help. If you trust in your ability to make it better later, you may be more willing to lower your standards on the first draft and accept that the draft will be (temporarily) awful. That willingness will keep you from getting hung up and blocked, as often happens to writers who feel that they *must* start with the perfect first paragraph. Think of how much time you could save, how much stress you could shed, if you could relax and spew forth a first draft, rather than agonize over every movement of the cursor.

As you come to value revision, you will find an almost infinite array of tools at your disposal. Some of them were developed as prewriting techniques, but now that many writers compose directly on a computer as soon as they get an idea, these methods of focusing, expanding, and collecting have found new life as revision tools. After all, writing is almost never a linear process that starts with a title and marches directly to a conclusion, with never a backward glance. Instead, most writers take a few—or a few hundred—steps forward, then circle back and cut, expand, and revise. So an alert writer may be collecting new information even during the final polishing steps just before publication.

No one example or argument will transform a writer's revision attitude. But before we can hope to learn something new, most of us need to unlearn dysfunctional beliefs, the reasons we resist revision.

Resistance to Revision

We need to be convinced about the *why* of revision before we'll get very far on the *what* and *how*, so let's start by figuring out the roots of revision resistance. You may distrust revision because you feel that:

1. *Revision is trivial, the nitpicky correcting of superficial niceties.*
Revision *can* include editing and polishing, but it means, after all, reseeing, so in extreme cases (as you'll see later in this chapter) it can mean rescrambling every paragraph of a paper or throwing out everything except the conclusion. Naturally, if you think of revision as concentrating on surface errors, you'll dislike it; few people enjoy having to focus on their own mistakes.

2. *Revision is unnecessary.*
If you've been praised for writing you did the night before the deadline, you may think the whole idea of revising—messing with that "good job!"—is crazy. You probably get, at 2 A.M. the morning of the deadline, what Susan McLeod calls the "joy of completion," and you probably feel that any additional work would be drudgery (1997, 23).

But revision offers writers many things beyond more praise or a better grade—a deeper, sharper understanding of the subject, a satisfying sense that the ideas come across in the best possible way, a chance to clarify and perhaps change your opinions. Unfortunately, because good student writers often don't seem to need revision to write A papers, they may reap the benefits of revision more slowly than their less proficient peers, who learn that revision holds their only hope of getting an A or pleasing the boss. Sometimes only a kick in the teeth—a C on a paper or a caustic comment from a teacher, editor, or boss—will convince a writer that a good first draft is no longer good enough. I know a few writers—experienced journalists—who in effect revise in their heads and make very few changes in the first hard copy. For the rest of us, though, revision is as crucial as running a spellchecker.

3. *Revision makes things worse.*
It does, if you change just for the sake of changing. All writers need to keep their purposes and audiences in mind as they revise. Change only to make the phrase, sentence, paragraph, or paper more clear, concise, complete, compelling, or convincing. You may need readers—peers, teachers, family members, editors—to help you decide if a change is an improvement.

4. *Revision is wasted time.*
Time spent revising can feel like good money thrown after bad. But experienced revisers learn when and how to revise for maximum effect. And the satisfaction of getting it just right gradually teaches writers that revision is its own reward, worth doing even when publication or a better grade is only a remote possibility.

5. *Revision is drudgery; only the first draft is creative.*
Writers at all levels are susceptible to this myth. Susan McLeod, who studies writers and their emotions, explains, "With this kind of myth helping to shape our emotional reactions to writing, it is no wonder that many of us (not just students) get discouraged waiting for inspiration to strike, or that we resent having to revise our work if we feel inspiration has produced it" (1997, 41). In *The Craft of Revision*, journalist and writing teacher Donald Murray says, "The published writer knows it takes a great deal of practice to be spontaneous" (2003, 3). Revision can be so creative that the original idea, the seed, disappears in what novelist Bernard Malamud called "the flowers of afterthought."

6. *Revision is a sign of failure, and criticism a personal affront.*
Because of such feelings, it's difficult for some writers to see that for most of us revision is the only road to success.

7. *You don't have time to revise.*
If you tack hours of revision onto a painful, labored process of writing a first draft, you *will* feel that the writing project is taking up your whole life. But if you learn to count on revision for improving a sloppy draft, you'll spend less time anguishing over the first draft and may actually finish more quickly.

8. *You don't know how to revise.*
You're not alone. But that's why we've written this book—to help you learn how.

If you identify with any of these feelings about revision, you're not going to change just because I tell you it's a good idea. To become true believers—and practitioners—of revision, most writers need to witness the power and value of revision, understand why they're revising, and experience a revision process that clearly improves their own writing.

Seeing Is Believing

To create a more productive attitude toward revision, we need first to see for ourselves what revision can do. Examples of major, positive revisions abound in the world outside of writing: architects' revisions of their house plans, directors' revisions of their movies (now open to study because of extended home video versions of many movies), your parents' repainting of the kitchen to get the color right. As a music lover who brings a boom box to almost every class, I find the best models in musical revisions. They're everywhere and easy to find, especially in this era of sampling. Although other groups' remakes of popular songs give us hope because they can transform dull into dazzling, I learn the most about writing by examining Bob Dylan's revision of his own song "I Want You."

The original version of the song was probably the most popular track on what many consider Dylan's best album, 1966's *Blonde on Blonde*. Before I play it, we read the words and debate what kind of tone, tempo, and attitude the music should convey. (I encourage you to get a copy, download the words off the Internet, articulate your own reaction to the lyrics, then listen for yourself.) Most people read desperate longing in the words and predict that the music will be slow and pained, reflecting the desperation. When I play the original version, they're chagrined—it has a bouncy, catchy tune, probably the happiest-sounding song on the album.

Twelve years later, Dylan released a live version of the song from a concert in Japan. It's much slower, pained, with at times only a flute accompanying the straining voice. It certainly raises the possibility that Dylan eventually heard the words the way most lyrics readers do and changed the music to match. In any case, the revised version is radically different, and it helps us see that sometimes writers revise even when they don't have to, even when the earlier version is published and acclaimed.

Think of your own favorite music. Do you listen to bands that record different mixes of the same song? Do they do cover versions of songs that others have written? How are the versions different? Why do the cover versions seldom follow the originals exactly? It's true that cover versions often don't sound better to fans of the original, but they prove that revision is a creative impulse and that clever people think it's worth spending time to improve something, even something already very good.

Musical revisions are fascinating and demonstrate many aspects of the reviser's art, but since we're writing, not making music, we need to find models of writing revisions as well. To answer the question How does good writing come about? some writing texts now print two or more drafts of a single piece. Barry Wallenstein and Robert Burr's *Visions and Revisions* (2002) offers almost three hundred pages of drafts and variations of poems, many by famous poets. In his *Read to Write*, Donald Murray publishes drafts from several prose writers as well as seven different versions of Mekeel McBride's poem "Red Letters" and an essay by McBride on the process of writing the poem (1993, 116–31). McBride explains that observations, dreams, word sounds, even typos affect the evolution of a draft; her essay demonstrates that good writers revise more than many novice writers can imagine.

Most writers have their own favorite examples of professional revisions and learn from these drafts how to improve their own. We can also find useful demonstrations in the drafts of our peers. Friends who write well may assert that they don't revise, but if pressed, they can probably show you early drafts, copies littered with corrections and changes, papers they rescued and overhauled after first efforts went nowhere . . . or at least they can tell you about the computer files erased and written over countless times. Whenever you get a chance to talk to other writers about their work, ask how much rethinking the piece of writing went through and whether you can see the first draft. Almost always, good writing results not from inborn talent, something that few of us can claim, but from hard work and sweat.

As a writer as well as a writing teacher, I collect my own false starts and messy drafts to demonstrate that even experienced professionals never get it "right" the first time. The cycle of feedback and revision goes on at all levels. I hope this short paragraph is clear and simple and reads as though I wrote it quickly and effortlessly, but I've revised it at least ten or fifteen times, using as guides the comments of a dozen other professional writers.

The three versions of my poem that follow demonstrate radical revision, and I share them to help other writers get over the revision-is-proofreading misconception. The subject of the poem is simple—the importance of mail in the freelance writer's life. With a title borrowed from a Shirelles song and mailbox details that seem to go nowhere, "Please Mr. Postman," an early draft, is not an impressive effort. But the last image—of seeing your own name in your own handwriting on a self-addressed stamped envelope and knowing that it's another rejection—stuck with me. (Writers mail their work—their hope—to editors, enclosing an S.A.S.E. in which the editors can return the material with an acceptance or rejection. So if your living or identity rests on editors saying yes, those envelopes take on an almost Judgment Day importance.)

Please Mr. Postman

As I grow older
and my submissions to fate
even more desperate
my mail boxes—
fate's portals—
get further away.
I used to pluck hope

from the little black wall box
with one foot still inside
on the ground.
RFD boxes were a barefoot sprint away
breath held
anticipation sharpened
by the cold of grass or snow.
Now harvesting the mail
requires shoes
and a five minute suspension
of the day's despair.
The manila envelope
slotted inside the office supply catalogue
slices out
the paper cut deepens
the never-closed wound.
The rejection always comes
addressed by my own hand.

My writing group helped me see that the poem didn't work, but I was unwilling to give it up, so I expanded it to over a page, then finally, disgusted, cut it down to the single image that I and my readers liked. That led to the first version of "S.A.S.E."

S.A.S.E.

By my own hand
addressed and infected
the rejections fester.

Reasonably happy with it but unsure whether it could still be called a poem, I sent it off to *The Epigrammatist*, whose editor, Nancy Winters, responded that she liked the idea but wanted me to revise it and make it rhyme. For days I stomped around, reacting as my students probably react when they get back a paper with my comments—yelling at the editor, griping about the stupidity of rhyme, ranting, "It's only eleven words long; how can I revise it?" But when I finally calmed down and revised, I had to admit that the changed rhythm and new rhyme did help. Rather than cruelly thwarting my ambitions, the editor's comments actually prompted me to make the poem better than I could make it on my own. Winters accepted the revision, and "S.A.S.E." became one of my first published poems.

S.A.S.E.

By my own hand
addressed and infected
it festers, rejected.

Although I seldom know if such happy-ending stories truly affect writers' beliefs about revision, a similar story *did* work for Melanie. Because she's a musician, Melanie has always had a good attitude toward revision. She's been playing the violin seriously for years, spending thousands of hours going over and over the same passages, trying to get just the right nuance of revision to make the teacher smile, knowing that everything the teacher says is intended to help, to make it all sound better and be more fun.

But one moment in eleventh grade stands out for Melanie because it proved to her the value of extreme revision, of whittling down to the core. Melanie's English teacher, the disciplined and reserved Ms. S., opened up to students and endeared herself to Melanie by sharing a poem she had been working on for seven years. Melanie was astonished that the poem was only eighteen words long. At first, that didn't seem enough for all those years of work. But eight years later, Melanie can still recite every word of the poem. She's learned that sometimes in writing, as in music, less is more, and seemingly endless revision may produce something memorable.

Understanding

Demonstrations of revisions may convince writers like Melanie that they *should* revise, but they're of limited value in helping writers figure out *how* to revise. To learn how, we must first accept that revisers have reasons; revision is, largely, a rational process. Many young writers are confused by the conventions of English grammar and see writing as a mysterious game that only English teachers understand. These writers need to see that logic, imagination, and reason, not obscure rules, motivate everything writers do, every comment teachers and editors make. Writers who don't understand the reasoning behind critiques will, naturally enough, be reluctant to revise. So if you're going to revise successfully, it's critical to understand explanations of teachers', bosses', and editors' responses and to make sense of why you're revising.

Such an understanding was necessary to convince Jared about revision. Other teachers had told Jared that his sentences and paragraphs were too long, and he had always resented it. He's a sophisticated reader, well aware that critics praise, not condemn authors like William Faulkner and Samuel Beckett and their endless cascades of words. So the criticism, the prohibition on letting the clutch out on his sentences, struck Jared as arbitrary and unfair.

As had his other teachers, classics professor Mark Damen pointed out some whoppers in Jared's paper. But Damen made sure Jared understood what was wrong with the sentences, not by counting words up to an arbitrary maximum, but by showing how the sentences might be confusing, how an active verb here, some punctuation there, some trimming all over could quickly and easily improve the sentences. After absorbing Damen's comments on the paper, Jared talked with him one-on-one, and the professor's focus on improving the paper convinced Jared that they were working together. Damen was not punishing Jared for his errors.

Like Mark Damen, most people who respond to writing want to help writers improve their work—current and future—rather than penalize them for mistakes. But it's difficult to see that intent when the boss covers the memo with red ink or the teacher hands back a paper with a big D at the end. How can you move from the anger, frustration, and depression you're likely to feel at such a moment to an attitude that will make revision productive, perhaps even fun?

1. *Cool off.*
If you've already looked at the grade or general evaluation, there's probably no point in reading the comments right away. Rejection letters sometimes upset me so much that I can't really "hear" the editor's comments for hours, maybe days. It doesn't help to go through the comments saying, "What a lame thing to say, you loser."

2. *Try to give the responder the benefit of the doubt.*
If you read the comments looking for things that are wrong or stupid, you'll probably find them. But if you read them looking for suggestions that will actually make your paper better, you'll probably find them, too.

3. *Read the comments in context; they won't make sense unless you link them with the paper itself.*
Imagine yourself in the responder's place, reading the paper and making comments about specific things. Back up at least a paragraph and reread what you wrote, then read the comments. It sometimes takes me several readings to see what my words actually say and to realize that an editor really has found weaknesses in what I thought was a flawless passage.

4. *Ask the responder for further explanation.*
Make clear that you want to understand and to improve your paper. Most readers are delighted when writers value their comments.

5. *Use what's useful; disregard the rest.*
It's your writing. Most readers' comments are just suggestions, not orders. I follow most of my suggestions with (?), implying, "What do you think?" A suggested revision of a sentence tells you that there's probably a problem with the sentence and indicates one direction a revision might take. Use that information, build on it, but don't take it as a command.

6. *Applaud every little improvement.*
And don't try to do everything at once. If you find the process difficult and stressful, revise for only fifteen or twenty minutes at a time, or until you're convinced that you've made one substantial improvement. Then pat yourself on the back and do something else. With a draft and a reader's comments in hand,

you can return to the revision whenever you feel like it and work in very small increments of time.

7. *Let it go.*

There's nothing noble about endless revision. Before you start hating the paper, turn it in, send it off, file it. Don't subscribe to the myth that writing is torture. Revision is hard work, but you won't be doing yourself any favors if you push the revision so hard on one paper that you can't stand to revise the next one.

To understand and make use of feedback and revision ideas, we may need to change the metaphors that we use to think about revising. Writing metaphor expert Barbara Tomlinson would want us to wean ourselves from metaphors like *nit-picking* and *polishing* and start seeing revision in terms of what she calls "stories about hard labor and artistic processes," using metaphors like "refining, casting and recasting, painting, sculpting" (1998, 75). My poem "Eddie's Full-Service Rewrite" suggests one way to rethink such metaphors and offers a hierarchy of revision steps, from straightening the frame to polishing the chrome.

Eddie's Full-Service Rewrite

Revision is body work, overhaul
Ratcheting straight the frame
Replacing whole systems and panels
Rummaging heaps of the maimed.
With blowtorch and old rubber hammer
Pound and pull, bend, use your 'bar
Salvage takes sweat but it pays well
(Though never rule out a new car).

Through editing, tuning, adjusting
You get all the volts to the spark
Knock all the gunk from the filters
Set timing right on the mark.
Trade in your hammer for feeler gauge
Test drive and listen, hush!
A smooth-running engine's a miracle
Though mange mars the bucket seats' plush.

The proofreader's focus is narrow
The weary say "Why should I care
About snotballs of tar on the door here
Creases of rust over there?"
But oh! If the paint job's neglected
The whole thing will look like a mess
Stray commas pock bodies like acne
And threaten to rot out the rest.

Why strain your elbows on hood chrome
If the pistons stick, mired in glue?

No profit in setting the carb right
If the drive shaft is broken in two.
So when you're at Ed's contemplating
How to triage repairs on your wreck
Start with the frame and the engine
Don't waste your polish on dreck.

Almost every skill or process offers its own analogies to the process of revising writing, and writers who question the value of time spent revising might benefit from thinking about their own metaphors. How is creating a good recipe, learning to sail, developing a relationship, or growing a garden similar to revision? A history of successful revision in one of those areas might give writers the confidence to spend enough time revising their writing that they'll feel successful.

Successful Revision Experiences

Inspiring as Jared's and Melanie's stories are, I think Becky's and Brett's are more common. Both learned to value revision by seeing sentence by sentence and idea by idea what it could do for them. Becky was in a class that required sharing drafts with a group of classmates, and the teacher encouraged group-mates to tear each other's papers apart. Though I cringe at that metaphor—I want peer readers to take the process seriously, but not to use claws—many students report that the right mix of peers can create a relaxed atmosphere of honest feedback and creative sharing, with revision the product, the goal.

Brett's high school poetry teacher was willing to give up her lunch hours to read students' poems, and Brett had enough initiative to write poems and take them to her. He didn't always agree with her responses or like her suggestions, but most of the time he saw that the poem was better by the end of lunch hour, and he became a long-term fan of revision.

Despite all the convincing demonstrations of revision and explanations about how it can work, we probably won't change our attitude about it until we successfully revise our own writing, finding a more interesting focus, a more unusual perspective, a peppier verb. No one can give you such an experience; it has to come about as a result of your own work on your own sentences. But almost any writing teacher, hundreds of books on writing, and even some word-processing style checkers can point you to passages that can benefit from reworking, give you suggestions about reorganization, list focusing questions.

The rest of this book describes ways that teachers and students, readers and writers have worked together to create positive revision experiences, to get over that crucial hump to "Yes, this works. It's worth it." Practiced revisers can work almost simultaneously on scores of processes, from checking homophones to rethinking theses. But I find that simple, step-by-step approaches can best open writers' eyes to the value of revision and lead us to make major changes without thinking, "I'm revising."

One of my favorite step-by-step approaches is the descriptive outline (see Appendix on page 12). It helps writers resee what they've done, revealing where their emphasis is and how they can change it. It enables writers to identify where crucial transitions need to be and therefore helps them achieve a seamless train of thought. My hope is that after following the descriptive outline, or using any of the other suggestions in this book, writers will begin to see revision not as another tedious burden, but as the writer's best friend, something you can count on to improve the writing, the response, and your feeling about it. Someday you may even agree with columnist Ellen Goodman, who said, "What makes me happy is rewriting."

Works Cited

Dethier, Brock. 1994a. "Eddie's Full-Service Rewrite." *English in Texas* 25 3: 43.

———. 1994b. "S.A.S.E." *The Epigrammatist* 5 3: 16.

———. 2003. *From Dylan to Donne: Bridging English and Music*. Portsmouth, NH: Heinemann.

Ericksen, Brett. 2002. Interview by author. September. Logan, UT.

McLeod, Susan H. 1997. *Notes on the Heart: Affective Issues in the Writing Classroom*. Carbondale, IL: Southern Illinois University Press.

Murray, Donald. 1993. *Read to Write*. 3d ed. Fort Worth, TX: Harcourt.

———. 2003. *The Craft of Revision*. 5th ed. Fort Worth, TX: Heinle.

Omer, Melanie. 2002. Interview by author. September. Logan, UT.

Songer, Rebecca. 2002. Interview by author. September. Logan, UT.

Tomlinson, Barbara. 1988. "Tuning, Tying, and Training Texts: Metaphors for Revision." *Written Communication* 5 1: 58–81.

Wallenstein, Barry, and Robert Burr. 2002. *Visions and Revisions: The Poet's Process*. Orchard Park, NY: Broadview.

Woolstenhulme, Jared. 2002. Interview by author. September. Logan, UT.

Appendix

Goal: To resee the paper, its parts, and its connections and to focus revision on issues of content and organization.

Descriptive Outline

1. Number each paragraph. This is the only thing you do on the paper itself. Part of the point of this activity is to take attention away from the individual pages of the paper and focus it on the skeleton you're about to construct. It's much easier to get a sense of the whole when it's all on one page.

2. On a clean sheet of paper, jot down a number for each paragraph, spacing evenly (i.e., if you have twenty paragraphs, number the paper 1–20).

3. Summarize each paragraph in as few words as possible. Write each summary next to the appropriate number.

4. Reflect on what you just did. Why were certain paragraphs difficult to summarize? Are they unfocused or incoherent or compound? Should you break a paragraph into two? Did you find you could use ditto marks because a number of paragraphs in a row were about the same subject? Does the subject deserve that much attention? Could someone glancing at the summaries of your opening and closing paragraphs get a sense of how they connect?

5. Group the summaries into blocks. Use brackets or different colors or whatever works. First get every summary into a group, then bracket some of those groups into larger blocks until you get to the one block that they all fit under. Label each group.

6. Reflect again. Are some summaries out of place, requiring you to draw an arrow to the correct group? Does the number of paragraphs in each block roughly correspond to the relative importance of that block? You have now created a kind of an outline sometimes called a tree diagram. Do its major blocks correspond to what you see as the major sections in your paper? Are you missing parts? Do the blocks appear in the best order?

7. Mark junctions between blocks and summarize what the transition at each spot needs to do. Between every pair of blocks, big and small, there should be some indication of a change of subjects: a paragraph break or a bullet if not some kind of verbal transition. Resist the temptation to see what transition you *did* use. First figure out what *should* be there, then see if you can find it in the paper.

8. Write down all the changes you want to make.

This process in effect X-rays the draft, and this new form of seeing can open your eyes to many kinds of revision, not just organizational problems.

Two

Revising Out and Revising In

Wendy Bishop

You must demolish the work and start over. . . . It will be a miracle if you can save some of the paragraphs, no matter how excellent in themselves or hard-won. You can waste a year worrying about it, or you can get it over with now. (Are you a woman, or a mouse?)

The part you must jettison is not only the best-written part; it is also, oddly, that part which was to have been the very point. It is the original key passage, the passage on which the rest was to hang, and from which you yourself drew the courage to begin.

—Annie Dillard

Annie Dillard describes a writer's not unnatural hesitation to revise, particularly when doing so means abandoning key points, the ones that started the journey, the ones that took energy and courage to organize on a page. Her remarks also suggest that in order to revise, you must have a wealth of hard-won material in your computer file that you'll shape in order to suit your final aims. When a reader suggests, "Your essay *really* starts here," and points to the second or third paragraph, it's tempting to ignore the suggestion and walk away. As Dillard observes, you can waste another week trying to make that initial paragraph or idea fit . . . or you can go ahead and see what happens when you start with paragraph 3 and explore, reshape, and complete your text.

Many authors rush to finish a piece of writing. The nearer they are to projected end points, the more eagerly they look forward to stopping. Due dates, page limits, genre expectations, any number of *extrinsic* goals—goals imposed by others—can fuel this writerly sprint despite our understanding that the draft would benefit from more exploration, risk taking, and play. Of course, *intrinsic* goals—those writers set for themselves—also influence revision. Invested writers make the task their own through self-challenges like deciding to create a hypertext version or trying formal argument because it's been a weak point in their repertoire. Without tension, expectations, and self-challenges, a writer will likely remain disengaged with the text, with the entire project, with the expectations others have for that particular piece of writing.

We may accept deadlines—but we make them our own when we commit to them for our own reasons as well. When writers ask task setters, "How long should this be?" they are likely asking themselves, "How much do I want to devote to this project? Is it worth my time, and if so, how much?"

Certainly the pace of contemporary life turns all authors into pragmatists and multitaskers. Most of us work under deadline pressures and on more than one piece of writing at a time. We have to learn to be efficient in order to keep up. But there's a danger when we learn to conserve energy (we think) by investing too cautiously, by doing just enough but rarely much more. The result? We write two thousand words *and only two thousand words* because two thousand is the minimum and the paper is soon due. How can we revise when we've left no room for instructive mistakes, when removing text means throwing away what we've barely just completed, when cutting out an ineffective paragraph means failing to meet a required minimum? We don't. Our initial low investment leads to continued low investment: we hang on to an early thesis (even though the actual paper has developed in a slightly different direction) because—by gosh—it's a good thesis and they're hard to write. And so on.

"Waste not" is an efficient product-producing motto. It's less easy to see how "Be wasteful" may be even more efficient. For instance (at a microscale): *You can't waste not without having something to waste, until you have been generous, reckless, and profligate with your drafting, until you've revised out, making your text 25, 50, 100 percent longer than you envisioned the final product as needing to be* (forty-one words).

How did I know if the previous sentence needed the word *generous* or *reckless* or *profligate*? I didn't worry; I listed what came to mind, knowing I could choose later. When I had captured the direction of my thought, I returned, played and tinkered with the text, changing, cutting, reordering. I needed to revise out before I could revise in: *The best way to avoid waste in writing is to be generous when drafting, to revise out, to make your text longer before making it effectively shorter* (twenty-seven words). Having traded in forty-one words for twenty-seven, I began to discover my message. (And I have to admit that I revise both sentences, like I revise all of my sentences, each time I read them again.)

On Drafting Generously

By drafting generously, writers discover not only what they might mean to say but also more ways of saying it—some of which they'll like, some of which they won't. Revising out allows for revising in and often helps a writer as a result produce a better text because all investigations—of ideas, words, sentences, style, shape, and tone—are instructive to the interested writer. Consider John Updike's claim: "Writing well involves two gifts—the art of adding and the art of taking away. Of the two, the first is more important, since without it the second could not exist."

Some more claims, explored in this chapter:

* Drafting recklessly makes writers feel rich, keeps them from hoarding; trusting that they have more ideas to come, they develop *flexibility*.

* Drafting generously allows writers to ignore internal and external critics who claim first drafts are best, extra words are wasted words, *good* writers get it right the first time, and so on. *Invested* writers try and tinker. Incessantly. They study options and experiment with them on the road toward becoming *modestly expert*.

* Drafting out in order to draft in takes advantage of the inventive, cyclical, recursive nature of composing. Flow is followed by ebb, ebb by flow. Considering global (ideas, organization, etc.) as well as local issues (style, conventions, etc.) repeatedly, sometimes simultaneously, strengthens an author's ability to *tolerate ambiguity* and *avoid premature closure*.

Perhaps you already have the ability to be flexible while drafting, to explore choices, to balance modesty with expertise, to tolerate ambiguity in order to enlarge your drafting options. But if you're like me, it's a constant challenge to do these things. That's why writers swap advice and offer their own best practices up for examination. The exercises that follow do the same.

Got Text?

To arrive at the end of an initial draft—what I call a full-breath draft—is your first goal. Perhaps this happens during a drafting high, a keyboard flow, fingers keeping up with your racing thoughts. But for every drafting sprint, there are times when any writer slows and stops well before the finish, thinking: "I didn't choose the right topic," "If only I had started earlier," or "I wasn't in the mood and, besides, I don't like the assignment." Despite wanting to write, writers may lose their forward motion and fail to arrive at their drafting goal.

At this point, most of us invest heavily in false hope, sometimes going as far as imagining the first draft can stand in for the final draft. "Maybe it's enough," we say to ourselves, or "Just let my readers get to the second page, then it starts rolling," or "I hope they don't notice the way the second scene doesn't really fit, since that's the only scene that's working, and I can't dump it." It's equally easy to talk ourselves into Quitters' Corner: "That's all I have to say," or "It's good enough for a pass/fail psychology assignment," or "To do all that, I would have to write a book!" Self-justification boils down to a predictable litany of excuses: "If I had more energy (time, interest, support, food, a better boss, a better computer, etc.), I could do a better job."

When draft bogs down or enthusiasm wanes too quickly, it's time—actively, as a self-assignment—to revise out because, in your heart of hearts, you know you need more material to work with. You can't buy the minimum amount of fabric suggested for a sewing pattern because you might make a mistake cutting it out and need more. You don't take three days' worth of food on a three-day camping trip, you take extra. If you invite five for dinner, you cook to feed eight, and your closet holds more than a week's clothing although you wash your clothes every week. Students envision exam questions; runners travel past the finish line (not just barely up to it); travelers scoop up more CDs than they can possibly listen to on a flight; and shoppers withdraw extra cash from the ATM (if they can), just in case. Why, oh why, do we overprepare in so many areas of life but not in writing? In fact, would you credit it—I orginally generated twice as many examples as you see in this section alone, in part because being extravagant is fun. And certainly I could still cut more (for instance, most of us no longer sew our own clothes, so it's likely that analogy is wasted). Remember, everyone loves a big spender. And, luckily, words don't get totaled up on a composition credit card bill.

To have options in revising, you have to get text. An abundance of it. Here are two initial ways to arrive at greater fullness:

1. Write a fat draft. Double your text. Toss out your internal critic because this writing doesn't have to be impressive, it simply has to be there. Measure roughly by pages or precisely by word count.

2. Write a memory draft by rereading your text carefully, preferably aloud. As you do, pay intense attention to your topic and ideas. Put that draft out of sight, open a new file on your computer, and compose the piece again. Make this version at least as long or longer than the original. Do not at any time consult the original draft.

In each case, your goal is to draft out, to get text, to create additional material. Compile a rich, high-calorie, high-octane fat draft or discover alternate ways of developing your ideas within the reflective and exploratory spaces of a memory draft. If you can, do both; write the fat draft and then from that version compose a memory draft; compose a memory draft and then double that draft length. Eventually, you can combine versions into a new, expanded draft ripe for revising in.

These assignments aren't tricks. They're techniques many writers discover for themselves. Nicole began her fat drafting by responding to peer critique:

> I sat again at my computer and took out the drafts that were commented on by my group members. I incorporated new sections in response to their suggestions but still found myself running short of doubling my draft. So I sat there pretty blank and typed some nonsense. Then I pushed away from what I was actually writing and went back to some childhood memories that related to my "theme" on literacy for my paper on speaking out. I began to write about that and my paper became a little more visual and fun again. I started to show instead of tell—like I did in the beginning.

Weeks later, while writing another essay, Nicole couldn't find her full-breath draft in her computer files. She forced herself to sit down and rewrite the original text from memory (because those two thousand words were due the next day). The next morning, working at her computer again, she found the original file and printed it out and brought both drafts to class. Nicole had invented the memory draft for herself and she was quite excited by what she learned in comparing the two versions—she explained that things she thought important in the first draft had faded. In the memory draft, different events took on significance and she discussed them in unexpected detail. For her final draft, Nicole used material from both versions.

I use the term *fat drafting* humorously because contemporary U.S. culture conditions us to "think thin," which in writing often means too skinny, under-developed, or meager. Fat drafting encourages writers to add significant detail, to explicate ideas, and to explain what they thought might not be needed by a reader (but so often *is* needed). Memory drafting asks writers to trust that what's truly important—most salient—will remain available for further exploration. Memory drafting encourages writers to abandon the fluff, filler, and fussy details that pad any draft when it is being dragged toward minimum length. Used together, the exercises help a writer develop *and* refine—twin goals of mid-level drafting. At this point the writer is beyond rough draft but not yet ready for editing and proofreading. Given time, writers could stay in this instructive, idea-generating middle space of thinking through writing for a great deal of time. Perhaps it's time to revise in.

On Becoming Your Own Expert

Authors in this collection—particularly in Chapters 3 and 4—offer their readers ways to know themselves as revisers. They base this advice on their own writing experiences and on their familiarity with research into the habits of expert and novice writers that has been available since the late 1970s. Novice writers tend to write too little. If they compose at greater lengths, they may do so with little reflection or connection (while a fat draft expands on an idea, a rambling text never comes to any point). Both sorts of writing fail to consider the needs of readers. Those who write too little, who feel blocked or worried, are often afraid of making mistakes, of spelling words wrong, of being judged inexpert, of failing at an assignment . . . again. Because writing is often bound up with our self-image, it's wise to remember that we can all be turned into novices by unexpected or unfamiliar writing conditions and tasks.

Expert writers, on the other hand, have developed an understanding of their own writing abilities. They are flexible composers who tolerate ambiguity as they explore their ideas, and they revise at many levels. Sometimes they revise globally—radically reorganizing their text or tossing a draft out and starting again (as in the memory draft); they also rework their writing by reordering, subtracting, and adding—paragraphs, sentences, and words. Expert writers may not leave a recognizable drafting trail. They've internalized many skills and do a great deal of work in their heads, before committing to paper. Seemingly, they are single drafters, but in-the-head drafting, too, requires revision. No matter their preferred habits, professionals are willing to produce more text than they need if doing so allows them to make strategic decisions and revise writing to their own satisfaction.

Although they weren't included in the research studies I've summarized, John Updike and Annie Dillard offer advice based on their own experiences as experts. Like Updike, we want to develop the ability to revise out in order to revise in—utilizing the twin gifts of adding and taking away. Like Annie Dillard, we need to give ourselves pep talks: avoid unproductive worry, feel like writing men and women (not like mice), and learn not to hang on to a good word, sentence, structure, or idea too long. Like both these writers, we can learn these lessons more fully through revision exercises that you'll find in the Appendix on the following page.

Appendix

Approaches to Revision

These exercises echo some of those shared in other chapters of this collection, since one technique often suggests another.

Exercises in Section 1, "Getting There," provide options for opening up your draft to greater length.

Exercises in Section 2, "Being There," provide methods for exploring, experimenting, and playing with a draft.

Exercises in Section 3, "Beyond the Call of Duty," take you further with revision than you might have expected to go.

Exercises in Section 4, "With a Little Help from Your Friends," review ways for training yourself to be a better reader of your own drafts and for making use of readers' responses while you revise.

Exercises in Section 5, "On Beyond Zebra," allow you to investigate your openness to collaboration and coauthoring.

Although these exercises are presented in categories that roughly correspond with the early, middle, and late stages of drafting a text, such an organization is presented for convenience only. Don't be afraid to try revising out any option at any time. As mentioned earlier, during the life of a text, writers regularly alternate between global and local concerns. Besides, the best revision techniques are the ones that help you rethink and rewrite your draft so that you're happier with the end result.

Section 1: Getting There

To get more text:

1. Highlight the center-of-gravity sentence in each paragraph of your draft. This is similar to but not the same as composing a descriptive outline, which asks that you create a new summarizing sentence for each paragraph (see Chapter 1 Appendix). Peter Elbow suggests that the center-of-gravity sentence in freewriting is that sentence which calls attention to itself, seems core, crucial, provocative, evocative, and so on. In a new file, list these sentences and use them as writing prompts that let you write more deeply into your current text.

2. Choose one of the new paragraphs, completed in exercise 1, to begin a memory draft.

3. At the end of each day of drafting a text, write down what you'd do to this draft if you had one more hour, one more day, one more week, and one more month to compose and revise. As you begin the next drafting session, start by reading these notes to help you reenter the draft.

4. Focus down in order to expand out. Instead of covering a broad sweep

of time or jumping from place to place—four years of high school; all the events of a complicated divorce; everything published on California beach erosion over the past five years; the fine-grained history of an obscure band—compose a close-up. Instead of years, cover weeks; instead of days, consider one day; instead of trailing after your topic, locate your speaker, narrator, character, subject, issue in one particular place and time.

5. Instead of a fat draft, which entails a bit of freewriting and sometimes unmindful expansion, expand more mindfully. Add a paragraph (or stanza) between each paragraph (or stanza) that already exists. If you have only one paragraph, add a new sentence between each old sentence and see what that expanded paragraph *tells you* to write next. (Crawl if you must, but crawl. Soon you'll pull yourself up and start running.)

Section 2: Being There

If you have what I call a full-breath draft—the full conception—enough material so that others might profitably respond to your writing *without* you saying, "Oh, I was going to add that later," you're ready to make what you say more thoughtful, richer. The draft is conceptualized but in no way final. Time to experiment, explore, risk, play.

6. If you use an opening quote or an interview quote or a citation, contextualize it more fully. Let your voice introduce the material and move from the contributing voice back to your own idea development, and/or paraphrase the material so all the ideas (with proper citations) are presented by you. If you haven't already, discuss the formerly cited idea for another paragraph: What do you think about it? Most of us tend to throw interview quotes and expert opinion into our writing like rocks into a pond. Refloat those rocks, put the other voices *in dialogue* with your own thinking and commentary.

7. Insert subtitles into your text. This is as if you were inserting key headings from an outline into the text. Before and after each subtitle, develop reader-friendly transitions: consolidate what you said in the section you are ending and forecast what's coming in the next section. As you actually move past the subtitle into the next section, open by forecasting what is to come in this section and provide a bit of connection to the overarching point(s) of your whole text. In doing this, think of yourself talking to a friendly, interested listener. Later, if you wish, you can remove the subtitles, although you may decide you want to retain them. (Stage directions work similar organizational magic for screenplays, as do frame stories for narratives.)

8. Write a contrasting paragraph to each assertion you made in your draft—turn some unexpected corners.

9. Insert a list into your text and then explore the items in the list. Instead of using the list to compress an idea, use it to open up ideas.

10. Find two places in the current draft where expansion would be welcome. Write into those areas for a while, even if you feel like you're going on tangents.

11. Two days after finishing your first full-breath, shareable, draft, copy your conclusion to a new file and write two pages, using this conclusion to begin your new draft. When working with a research paper, resist including any quotes. Now that you're more learned and expert about your subject, try to detail your points in your own words (you can include and attribute sources later). If you can't do this, you have a clue that the sources in your full-breath draft may be shoring up a discussion that you don't really understand.

12. After you've moved from a full-breath to what I call a professional draft (one shaped fully enough that readers can offer substantive reflective and critical revision ideas), write informally about your subject twice each day for the next three days. Each time, open a new file. As you complete this exercise, think about your *topic,* not about your writing, as you go about your day. You can talk about your topic to others. You can read about it (in print texts and online), you can conduct interviews, but all this work should take the form of informal thinking and reading (keep a reference trail, though, just in case).

13. If you can, at the same time(s) each day—for me that might be 7 A.M. and 6 P.M., for you that might be 1 P.M. and 1 A.M.—upload your thinking. After three days, print and read the uploads, looking for material that will help you expand and focus your draft. If you have less time available before the writing needs to be completed, think-write three times in one day and revise the next day. You're trying to allow for as much mindful, off-draft percolation as possible.

Section 3: Beyond the Call of Duty (Perhaps? Perhaps Not?)

To expand your revision skills, try one of these exercises. Some of these exercises lead to long-term insights rather than immediate results.

14. *Play chorus director.* If you have produced a mono voiced text, find five to ten other voices that could be used in your piece of writing, for example, newspaper stories, interview quotes, aphorisms or proverbs, historical data, research citations, lines from a TV show, or billboard copy. For each, freewrite in response to the other text. Decide if the quote, the freewrite, or both might effectively be used to expand and complicate your draft.

15. *Play transition cop.* Highlight your transitions. Footnote each with an explanation of how each transition (word, phrase, or even paragraph) functions in this text. Look for predictable patterns and try to alter them in conventional and unconventional ways. Review the highlighting to identify overtransitioned sections and undertransitioned sections. Decide if you want to even these out. Think about the ways repetition (of words, phrases), rereferencing someone or something or an earlier example, or the expansion of a metaphor might provide helpful continuity for a reader.

16. *Play translator and explicator.* Take the same transition-highlighted text and delete all the word and phrase transitions. Note where you are using those transitions to connect and indicate a movement from one related idea to the next and where they function to *cover up* an unsolved writing problem or smooth over an abrupt change of direction. At those spots, add a full paragraph to help your reader move through the text. Add discussion so that mechanical transition words and phrases can be avoided.

17. *Play devil's advocate.* As you read each paragraph of your essay aloud, insert a footnote at paragraph's end and type in a counterargument, comment, correction, amplification, or "What if?" question directed toward you, the writer. Alternate version: For each paragraph, note a connection or memory triggered by what you have just read and/or compile a list of possible resources or places to go (primary and secondary, or stylistic!) for amplifying the work of that paragraph. The next day, consider the footnotes: What do they tell you? Which paragraphs need the most work and of what sort? Dig in.

18. *Deepen your insights.* Highlight five provocative words in your text. Freewrite on each one until you can't (gasp) write any longer. Do the same with five sentences from your text. Do the same with five quotes related to your text (you might do these freewrites over three days). Consider whether this off-the-record expansion could be recycled into your text.

19. *Call on the world.* Collect five media images—ads, family photos, sound bites, and so on—that illuminate your text in some way. Freewrite in response to each of these (and in relationship to your text). Insert written (perhaps even visual) material from this exercise into your text.

20. *Take advantage of titles (and images and metaphors).* Write four solid titles for the text you have in hand (often these can be found by looking for a crucial word, phrase, or sentence in the text). Each title should be significantly different from the others. Make four copies (files) of your draft. Revise the opening and closing paragraph in each version in a way that helps to help make sense of the title and lets the title make

more sense of your text. Compare the versions—the four files. For the one you like best, continue to revise the remainder of the text to see if the title/metaphor/image can be more fully woven through and/or better support your text.

21. *Enjoy the company of others.* Add another human to your text, no matter the genre. Let his addition complicate and open up your text. (Try, as well, adding an animal, a plant, weather, a time of day.)

22. *Give your text (physical) voice(s).* Add dialogue to your text, no matter the genre. Let the addition of quoted, spoken words complicate and open up your text.

23. *Interrogate absence.* Investigate the space between larger units of your text: paragraphs, stanzas, sections, chapters, acts, and so on. Make a duplicate of your text and write into these spaces. Begin, perhaps, by inserting another structure: a single sentence, a headline, a poem stanza (for prose), a quote, an inner voice, and so on. The next day, consider which, if any, of these interrogations provides a useful expansion or link. Remove all those that don't work or write full paragraphs to further incorporate any that have still unrealized potential.

24. *Make use of expert strategies.* Find four examples that you like of the genre of text you're composing. These might open in very different ways (with a quote, with a joke, with statistics, etc.); revise your opening paragraph to echo the four experts you've found. What does each new paragraph "predict" you will need to change in your entire text? If some of these predicted changes offer you expansion ideas, incorporate them into your most recent draft.

25. *Learn from your text.* Highlight any terms, concepts, or ideas that could be difficult for your reader. Use the World Wide Web to track down definitions, articles on, descriptions of, and visuals of these items. (Reference books, if you have them handy, are very useful as well—visual dictionaries, catalogs, dictionaries, synonym finders, and so on.) If you mention hibiscus, learn more about hibiscus; if you're talking about a referee's decisions, try to find out more about referee decisions that changed games and careers; if you're arguing for the preservation of endangered plants or animals, spend some time studying images of and data about these plants and animals and also visit sites that appropriate or devalue the animal for commercial gain or argue against preservation. Interview experts. For your text, create an extended personal glossary. Then decide if any of that information could be used in your next draft.

26. *Ask and answer questions.* If you haven't yet, introduce three focusing (rhetorical) questions at different points in your text. Answer each at some length. Decide if you should leave the question and answer or remove the question and incorporate some of the answer into your text.

27. *Take it to the limit.* Draft your text to pieces. (This technique is particularly useful for shorter texts, troublesome paragraphs, and poetry.) Every time you turn on your computer, create a new file for the latest draft of this text: Revision1.doc, Revision2.doc, Revision3.doc. Continue doing this until you've created so many drafts you've finally "ruined your paper." Flip back through the drafts until you sense your writing regaining its integrity. Save this draft in a new file (Soliddraft1.doc) and revise it in, using any ideas in this book that help.

28. *Au contraire.* If you're at the point where you don't or shouldn't care about readers, try actively distrusting them in order to be more experimental. After a response session, remove everything that two or more respondents said they found effective and that you find (1) ineffective, (2) too much like what you always do in a text, and/or (3) is something you'd label "safe writing." Revise out beginning with what remains.

29. *Con amigos.* If you're at the point where you do and should care about readers, after a workshop make as many of the changes as you can in your draft that two or more respondents suggested (when there is an equal disagreement, you decide; when more agree than disagree, go with the majority). Consider which results you should retain. (See Chapter 10 for a similar exercise using poetry, which prompted my version of this exercise.)

30. *Thinking beyond the page.* Use colored markers on a print copy or color font on a computer copy to indicate where you'd create links if you were converting your work to hypertext. Then, compose these links *textually*, that is, provide the text that a reader would find if she clicked on that link. Finally, consider if some of this material might benefit your print text as inserts, sidebars, definitions, footnotes, endnotes, or appendices. If you can, continue on to compose a hypertext version and consider how closely it does or does not follow the original print version.

31. *Thank you, thank you very much.* Create a process-acknowledgment page and thank (in detail and in relation to your final product) all human or textual helpers—those with whom you talked about your paper, those who offered a useful revision suggestion, the dictionary that provided definitional input, and so on. Instead of a narrative page, footnote or endnote a draft to provide this information.

32. *Showcase process and product.* Make a casebook out of your text. Collect all the materials you used—perhaps by scanning the original sources—and narrate and illustrate their use. Why did you choose to use the quote by so and so? What led you to this image? Or, think of yourself posting all these materials on the wall in a writing museum. Now write the notes that would be posted next to each piece if you were curating the collection.

Section 4: With a Little Help from Your Friends

Writers need the pleasures of arrival and of sharing their work with receptive audiences. Be open to advice, because you're always in control of the revision decisions you make for your text. At first you can't even see what needs revising. Then you may be able to identify your problems (with the help of your readers), but you may not yet have the skill to make the needed or best changes. Eventually, you improve at detecting *and* correcting at both the global and the local levels. A lifetime of writing may be sufficient for this! When readers aren't available, you can learn to impersonate your intended or ideal audiences. A portfolio of collected works allows you to produce a representative selection of your work, prepared with readers in mind. As you work toward portfolio-quality revisions, try the following exercises:

33. Write a memo from the boss of revision to your draft. This boss will poke hard, looking for places you've been insincere, or fudged the work, or tried more than you could accomplish but weren't willing to admit it, and so on. Use these insights to revise in.

34. Write a letter from your ideal reader telling you, in detail, and by quoting from the text, what he likes about your draft. Use these insights to try to do more of what *is* working and less of what *isn't* working.

35. If you present only one view in your essay, make a list of other viewpoints that could be or should be taken into account. Choose two of these and explore your topic from those points of view (one full page each). You may want to incorporate some of this material and/or acknowledge these points of view in your portfolio draft.

36. Find a published writer you think does a solid job with a writing task much like yours (roughly on the same topic and for the same audience). Create a descriptive or post-outline for that essay or article—count how many paragraphs the writer uses, indicate the proportion of outside sources and support to author's opinion. What sort of support is used and where is it added? *Draw* the shape of the text in a way that lets you see its construction. Do the same for your own text. See if you can make your composition's structure and strengths more closely imitate those of your target text. (For other imitation exercises, see Chapter 4.)

37. Remove all the transitions from your prose. Print each remaining paragraph on a separate page and shuffle the pages. Ask two readers to read all the paragraphs and then arrange them in the order that seems most logical to them. If they differ in their ordering, from each other or from your original order, interview them to find out why. Revise using the best of your readers' reordering ideas, reinserting needed transitions.

38. Have a boring draft? Following too many rules? Not interested in the subject? Write yourself an Rx for your draft. As patient, list your

complaints, analyze your symptoms. As doctor, list three remedies for each problem (include sensible and experimental solutions). Revise by trying to follow two or three of the most provocative remedies.

39. For the opening and closing paragraphs of your draft, justify the inclusion and note the function of each sentence in the paragraphs by using footnotes. In these notes, defend your textual choices. The next day, look at your defense notes and revise any portion of the text for which you feel you're protesting too much or for which you have only lame justifications.

40. Alone or with other readers, examine your paper for connections that would strengthen it, then make a list and focus on those particular sorts of reweavings. To do this, consider connections between sentences (repeat words or variations on phrases to link and remind); create connections between paragraphs (refer back to previous discussions or forward to future discussions); connect characters or speakers or narrators; link sections and scenes; draw parallels via sentence patterns and syntax; and so on.

41. Read your text aloud to a listener who notes on her copy of the text all your miscues; these are places you changed what was on paper as you read aloud as well as places that you stumbled during your own oral reading (see Chapter 4 for more discussion of this technique). Review your partner's copy and discuss if changes are needed at those places. Prepare a plan for your final revision together.

42. Tell your writing group at some length (you should *talk*, without notes, for a minimum of five minutes) what you wanted to accomplish in the text, what you think you did accomplish, what points you were making and why, and who should read the essay and why. The group members take notes as you talk. Then they read your essay to determine how well you succeeded in your aims and to indicate where you might make final revisions in order to reach your goals.

Section V: On Beyond Zebra

As we become more expert, our writing strategies are internalized. That's useful. But we also internalize strategies that are efficient but not always elegant or we forget what strategies we rely on in a pinch. It's useful, when you can find time, to compare your habits with those of others, to make some of your revision processes visible again before you pack them away to use another day. Talking with other writers—sharing experiences and ideas—allows you to do this. As will the following two exercises.

43. Give two writing partners your first page (as a file). Ask them to use their word processor's *editing function* to track the changes they would make to this text if it were theirs. Even if they like your version, *they*

must make significant changes in your draft. Do the same to a copy yourself. Each of you prints out two versions: one where editing is tracked (example: Do the same to your own ~~a~~ copy of the draft ~~yourself.~~) and shows up visually on the original text and one where the text appears with the changes incorporated (example: Do the same to your own copy of the draft.). When you meet, line up the visible-editing drafts next to each other and the revised copies next to each other. Discuss what you see. Use any suggestions you wish, but your goal is to note down three of the *revision moves* others made on your draft that you might try on your next composition.

44. Choose a new writing trigger (a topic, data, a quote) and write your own short text, as will two to four other group members. Take these files and together compose a composite text (or each author can do this separately and the versions can be compared). About what portions of your original text—if any—did you feel ownership and not open to change? Did you find places where other writer(s) improved the text? As a group, share your feelings about solo and coauthoring and revising.

Three

The Masks of Revision

Hans Ostrom

Wherever you go, the adage says, there you are. The point seems to be that traveling in search of exotic experiences may not work because we filter them through lenses of our unchanging selves. After the filtering process, the new place looks about the same as previous places, and we might wonder why we bothered to leave home. A related point might be that if we really want a new experience, we might consider traveling inward to get to know ourselves better.

Restated for us writers, the adage might look something like this: Wherever your writing goes, it's still *your* writing. Or like this: However you revise your writing, the one revising is still *you*. That is, when told to revise—re-vise, revisualize—our work, many of us wonder how that's possible. Aren't we really reading our work with the same mind's eye each time? If so, how can we truly resee what we've written? The existence of creatures called editors implies that if we really want what we write to be seen freshly, we'd better call in a third party, a consultant, a hired hand—or a hired pair of eyes, to be more precise.

Allegedly, there are ways—not involving editors—to get around our same old selves and help us see our writing with figuratively new eyes. You know some of these ways as well as I, probably, and chapters in this collection contain any number of good ones. You may have someone or several ones read what you wrote and give you an honest response to it. Such a response isn't editing, but it might show you something to which you were blind and lead you to revise productively. If you're writing in and for a class, the instructor might serve as such a respondent, not just when she performs the ritual called grading, but before that, when you show her a draft. Small groups of other writers—inside and outside the class—can do the same thing. So can people who work at writing centers. Just hiding a draft from yourself for a while is supposed to help, too; when you pull it out of that drawer or out from under the couch or back up onscreen, you'll see things in it, about it, you didn't see before. That's the theory, anyway.

I'm all for these methods, have used them in my teaching and for myself, have seen many writers benefit from them. The methods' emphasis on revision as reseeing, as getting a fresh perspective, is worthy.

In the rest of this chapter, however, I'd like to explore another approach to revision. This approach springs less from the idea that a writer's single unchanging "self" needs help to negotiate perpetual blind spots, and it springs more from the idea that as writers, as persons, we have many selves. Whether this notion is truth, fiction, or simply a question of terminology (*self*, *selves*: what's the difference?) isn't terribly important, at least with regard to the revising I have in mind. I acknowledge that psychologists and others might claim the question is terribly important, but I also hasten to add that I'm using the notion of multiple selves loosely and figuratively, certainly not in the sense of Freud's ego, id, and superego or in the clinical sense of multiple personalities.

A recent study of college writers examined what students seem to believe about their writing and the writing process (Lavelle and Zuercher 1999). The authors of the study claim to have identified five types of "student-writing approaches." Do you see yourself—or your selves—in any of these categories? Take a look; here are the types:

1. *Elaborative.* Writers in this category view writing as very personal and concerned with elaborating on their beliefs and values.

2. *Low Self-Efficacy.* Writers in this category are wary toward, even fearful of, writing. They have serious doubts about their ability to write.

3. *Reflective-Revisionist.* The authors of the study viewed writers in this category as sophisticated, especially with regard to revision. Such writers revise a lot and rather like to revise their writing.

4. *Spontaneous-Impulsive.* As you might guess, writers in this category jump in and start writing, with no real plan. They may not be wild about revising, either.

5. *Procedural.* Writers in this category like to follow rules and guidelines, perhaps ones given to them by a teacher but also ones that might appear in a handbook. They like to know exactly what's expected, and their writing pays strict attention to these expectations. Sometimes they may see writing as just a job to be finished and may not have much true interest in what they're writing.

What do you think of these categories? When I looked at them, I saw myself and many writers I work with in them, but I also saw that, depending on the circumstances, I and other writers could fit into most if not all of them. Here is what I mean: When I write, I am in two or three categories at once. For example, I might be writing a personal essay that is elaborative, but I may be full of doubts about it (low self-efficacy), partly because I jumped in and started writing without a plan (impulsive), liked some of what I wrote but hated the rest, and might be very concerned about what the editor of a book or journal expects (procedural). After a few days, I may calm down, become more patient, and get into the swing of revising (reflective-revisionist).

I've seen writers I've worked with exhibit different characteristics during a single project—impulsive at one stage, lacking confidence at another stage, reflective and patient at still another stage. In other words, I like the categories and how they describe what many writers do, but I see approaches to and beliefs about writing as being extremely fluid, dependent upon what the author is writing, when, why, and for whom. This is another way of expressing the notion that we have many writer's selves at once—a *mixture* of beliefs about and approaches to writing.

How many of the categories mentioned here do you identify yourself and your writing with? First, review the categories. Relabel them to your liking, if need be. (I realize the terminology might make you a little dizzy, and the main thing to focus on is the notion of *different approaches to and beliefs about writing*.) If you had to place yourself in just one of the categories, which one would it be and why?

Now think about a recent writing project. To what extent did you, during that project, exhibit more than one of the characteristics described earlier? If you did exhibit more than one, think about why that was so, how you made the transition, and so on. You might even write a piece in your notebook—electronic or paper—about the different kinds of writer you are at different stages of a project or with different projects. That is, are you impulsive when you work on one type of writing but procedural (very concerned about rules and guidelines) when you write another? In this exploration, treat yourself as a subject of a study. Perhaps invent some labels that are more colloquial, even irreverent. Have some fun with the self-assessment, the working title of which might be "The Kinds of Writer I Am."

Given this backdrop of multiple selves and multiple student-writing approaches, I'd like now to concentrate for a moment not on how we *see, resee,* or *fail to see* when we revise our writing, but on what we *do* when we revise. I'd like to shift the discussion from *perception* to *performance* and discuss revision in a way that exploits, *makes use of,* the multiple selves, approaches, and beliefs.

The roots of drama—performing stories—in many cultures are connected with the use of costumes and, more specifically, masks. Masks and drama are linked in early cultures of Indonesia, India, Africa, North America, and Northern Europe, for example (Emigh 1996). Japanese Kabuki theatre involves masks, as does the stylized Italian commedia. The enduring symbols of theatre—a smiling mask and a frowning one—spring from the commedia tradition. Of course, masks quickly convey to an *audience* that a character or a creature different from the one wearing the mask is being represented, but they also enable the *performer* figuratively to lose himself in the character or creature represented. Ideally, during the performance both audience and performer get lost in the mask, temporarily believing that it is real. Although contemporary styles of acting seem to work from the inside out, developing character first and worrying about costume later, even some contemporary actors still prefer to start with the outside—the figurative mask—and work from there.

Let's assume that revising is not acting but that it does seem to ask us to shift from one self to another—from writer to reader, or from author to critic—and back again, and that it asks us to *perform* something in connection to the draft we have produced. Starting with these assumptions, I'd like to consider what masks we might figuratively put on when we revise so that we can take the most appropriate revising action. We certainly don't want to turn revising into melodrama, but at the same time, some *conflict*, which is the basis of drama, does seem to exist in the process of revision; that is, when we start to revise, we're located in a conflict between what we have written (a draft) and aspirations—our own and others'—for that draft: a better text that doesn't yet exist. What masks might we put on to help us negotiate the conflict most effectively? What follows are some possibilities.

First Mask: The One Who Cares About Your Writing

It is easy not to care about one's own writing, even in the face of the logic that if authors don't care about their writing, then why should anyone who reads it care? If we don't like or understand the writing task, we're likely not to care. If we're not especially interested in the material, or if we're tired, or if we suspect that anything we write will be judged harshly, we're likely not to care. Maybe we just feel strongly that there are much better things to be doing than writing what we're writing.

So I think the first mask we might consider reaching for is the mask of the One Who Cares.

Start by at least pretending to care.

- Carefully and attentively read aloud what you have written.
- Look at words, phrases, and sentences with your full attention. If you're working on a piece of fiction, treat the characters as friends, even if, within the story, they are supposed to be unappealing. What do you like about these people as *characters in fiction*? If you're working on a shorter poem, care about every word, no exceptions. Lift each word as you would an interesting stone, and look at it. If you're working on an essay, treat each paragraph like another room in a house you are visiting. What's interesting about this room, and this one, and that one?
- Look at the whole draft with great interest, even though it has its flaws.
- Like a craftsperson building a new chair, look at the draft as a worthwhile work in progress.
- Remember: These are *your* words in this draft. Try to own them.
- *Give your draft the honor of your full attention.*

For example, what turned out to be the second paragraph of this chapter was very difficult for me to write. I knew I wanted to connect the adage (Wherever you go, there you are) with writing, but I had a terrible time phrasing the connection in a way I liked. I got angry with the paragraph and even ignored it, as if it were a misbehaving pet. But I returned to it. I cared once more. I came to view it as an important paragraph with some problems and went back to work on it. Later I got help with it from this book's editor. This troublesome paragraph had received the honor of my and the editor's full attention. When someone else cares about your writing, especially about parts of it that are problematic, it is much easier to care about it yourself. It's wonderful to hear praise for what works well in our writing, but it's more important to hear advice about what doesn't work well. When someone takes the time to think about a flawed part of your writing, you know he cares.

An assignment may frustrate you, the material may not intrigue you, but what you're looking at is not the assignment or the subject of the course; it is something you've created. It may need work. It may need a lot of work. But it needs your work, your best work, which is possible when you wear the mask of the One Who Cares. The mask will look very much like your face, but the brow will not be furrowed, the eyes will be clear and alert, and the overall effect will be one of generosity and acceptance. If you just don't know where to begin with revising a draft, try to begin by caring, by getting invested once more in what you're writing.

Second Mask: The One Who Is Difficult to Please

It is also possible to become smitten by one's own writing, to be so enthralled with it that it can appear to do no wrong. One assumption with which I'm familiar is that students of creative writing are more likely to exhibit this infatuation than are students writing essays, reports, or case studies (for example). In my own teaching, I have not found this assumption to be valid. Many poets and story-writers with whom I work have very little confidence in their writing and sometimes need to put on the mask of the One Who Cares. Conversely, many first-year composition students, possibly because they are used to receiving high marks in high school, tend to look upon their first drafts with loving eyes and jealously resent any suggestions for revision—in their first month of college, anyway.

In any event, if we tend to resist all criticism of our draft, or if, indeed, we tend to see a first draft as the last draft, we may need to reach for the mask of the One Who Is Difficult to Please. While revising, writers might wear this mask when examining particular parts of a piece.

- If you tend never to revise your first paragraph, accepting whatever first paragraph you happen to write, then be difficult to please as you reread it.

- Or be difficult to please when it comes to the structure of what you've written—the order of topics in an essay, the order of scenes or plot segments in a story or a narrative essay, how you set out evidence in a paper that's trying to prove a point.

- When it comes to your own writing, in what instances are you a pushover for what you've written? Are you more of a pushover in one kind of genre (e.g., poetry) than in another (e.g., essay)?

Here is what I regard as a classic instance in which this mask is useful. It's what I call "the real beginning." When I work with poets for two or three months, I see at least a dozen poems. With at least a third of these poems, after I read an *early* draft, I suggest cutting the first one to four lines, sometimes more, because the line following the suggested cut rings out as the *real beginning* of the poem. Often this revision has occurred to the poet or is expressed in her work group even before I give my comments. But often the poet needs to hear it from the group or from me because, like all writers, she is predisposed to like, and to try to keep, that first line or those first lines. They belong to her. It is difficult to get rid of them—at least until the quality of the real first line becomes apparent. In drafts of short stories, the second paragraph is often and uncannily the real beginning. In drafts of essays, hundreds of which I read each year, the first paragraph is often a throw away, something the writer wrote on the way to really getting started, a figurative clearing of the throat before the singer starts the song. Many writers *habitually* put on the mask of the One Who Is Hard to Please when they return to a draft and read the first lines, sentences, or paragraphs. If the first part, against the odds, pleases them, then fine, but it better be good!

Third Mask: The One Who Is Not Alone

Sometimes it's good to write in a bubble, not thinking about literal or figurative readers. Linda Flower, Peter Elbow, and people with less interesting last names who write about composition call this "writer-based" writing, and it can take the form of freewriting, notes, quickly written drafts, journal entries, and so on (Flower 1979; Elbow 1987). Especially early in the process of writing something, but also at later stages, not thinking of the audience (readers) helps ensure that writers aren't being so on guard and audience-aware that they clutch up and are unable to get things up on screen or down on paper. Writer-based writing is meant to be less self-conscious writing, not necessarily less self-aware, but less worried about making a mistake. Particularly while revising, however, allowing others back into the sphere of your writing can actually energize you, partly by giving real focus and purpose to your revising performance. Elbow and others call writing with an audience firmly in mind "reader-based" (1998).

Put on the mask of One Who Is Not Alone. Imagine readers of your writing, their expectations, assumptions, knowledge, and ignorance. With this mask on, you are no longer just revising—moving words around—but revising *for* someone. Looking through this mask, you're seeing your words as others might see them. You're able to ask,

- How will reader X respond to this scene?
- Will X want more here, less there?
- Might X misunderstand this or think that is too obvious?
- Especially in an explicitly persuasive piece, what possible objections to my claims might X make? Play the devil's advocate, or guess where the evidence might be weak or not explicitly linked to the claim.

Answering such questions can point to where and how you need to revise, and it can do so in clear, unambiguous ways. Knowing in general that there's something wrong with a draft doesn't exactly inspire revision. But knowing that *this page* is flawed for *this reason* because of how *this reader* will probably react invites revision, rewards it immediately. If you are showing the draft to a friend, to a classmate, to a teacher, or to someone in a writing center, then the reader is literally at your side. But when no one is literally at your side, you may put on the mask and imagine how a reader might respond to your writing.

Wearing the mask of the One Who Is Not Alone positions us somewhere between the One Who Cares and the One Who Is Hard to Please. We still care deeply about what we've written, but we are also committed to thinking about what the ones there with us—prospective readers—*expect from* and *need from* the writing. We are able to look inward (care about our own work) and to look outward (aim to please an audience) at once. Because we care, we aim to please the audience. Or, because we believe the audience exists and will read this writing, and will react to it, we care. I should add that aiming to please an audience isn't the same as doing everything to please an audience. You may suspect, for example, that part of your audience will disagree with an argument your essay is supporting. In your essay you will aim to please these audience members insofar as you will anticipate their objections and address the objections with reasonable counterclaims and evidence. You will not go so far as to agree with that part of the audience. That would please them, but it would betray the purpose of your essay.

Here is a concrete example of thinking about the audience: When I wrote first drafts of this chapter and summarized the different categories of writing approaches mentioned earlier (elaborative, low self-efficacy, etc.), the summaries seemed very clear to me. Rereading the draft with other readers firmly in mind, I realized the summaries needed to be simpler and more to the point. I made them so, but when someone else read the draft, she said they still made her a little "cross-eyed," so I worked on them again. If I'd just been writing the essay to myself, my audience (me) would have been delighted with the first draft and known exactly what I was talking about in those summaries. But I wasn't writing just for myself, and I had to remind myself of that obvious fact at some point during the process. Also, hearing from a reader that something I had written made her cross-eyed was enormously helpful criticism—straightforward and honest.

In a short story, we may know exactly what we mean when we describe a character performing some action. But if we think about how other readers may interpret those words, we may realize that the passage is very difficult to follow, that what the character physically is doing is unclear. In a poem, sometimes just one ill-chosen word can throw off the audience, and often it's a word we could have easily replaced with a better choice if we had imagined how an audience might have reacted. Clarification and precision can result from wearing the mask of the One Who Is Not Alone.

Fourth Mask: The One Who Loves Details

Think about a memorable performance: a recorded piece of music you think is wonderful, a favorite book or film, the best tennis match or basketball game you ever played—something like that. What exquisite details do you remember—something small but perfect that made you love this thing you love even more?

Of course, it's easier to appreciate the details in something we love and something that's finished than it is to care about the details in something we're in the process of writing. Many writers with whom I work, even as they realize that, cumulatively, a lot of small errors can drag a piece of writing down, don't take the time to sweat the details because sweating the details is just too tedious. I know that I often don't sweat the details—because I'm in a hurry, or because a self I shouldn't listen to assures me that the reader will overlook this typo or that someone else will clean things up somewhere down the road of editing and publishing.

To wear the mask of the One Who Loves Details is really to approach your writing as a kind of satisfying game. This mask is actually different from that of the One Who Cares because it is possible to care about your writing but still not be a detail person.

Your writing is a labyrinth. It contains typographical errors, errors in punctuation and grammar, choices of words that need to be rethought, little steps in logic that need filling in, a scene that needs some added detail. As you work your way through the labyrinth, you take great delight in noticing these flaws and fixing them—if you're wearing this particular mask, that is. Instead of serving the dreary, droning Lord of Punctuation, you are competing with yourself, trying to beat the game.

I've had the opportunity to watch teenagers play a lot of video games, and I'm amazed by how quickly they absorb the details of the games, search the Internet for codes that help them beat the games, know the minutest moves made possible by the controller, become alert to subtleties in the virtual landscapes of the games. They approach the games with real discipline: preparation, knowledge, a will to do well, attention to detail. To them the game is pleasurable work, not just play. I see similar behavior in students who get immersed in their own drafts, going way beyond just generally caring about their writing. I will see a student totally committed to her short story, for example, and her drafts will be covered in ink, as if she had just emerged from a frenzy of revision. She will care about punctuating the dialogue just right, not because she necessarily cares about arcane rules of punctuation or plans to become an English teacher, but because she is involved with the details of her story—how this character is saying something at this crucial moment in the story. She is not just playing halfheartedly at revision but working with pleasure, sweating the details. She is wearing the mask of the One Who Loves Details; she loves being in that labyrinth of revision, operating in the virtual landscape of her story.

When I was revising this chapter, I reconsidered the following sentence many times: How many of the categories mentioned here do you identify yourself and your writing with? For a long time, experts on English usage have suggested that in more formal writing, we shouldn't end a sentence with a preposition (*with*). I considered rearranging the sentence so as to move *with*, but I didn't like how the rearrangements sounded. Also, I thought the sentence was very clear as is. And I also thought of the famous quotation from Winston Churchill: "Ending a sentence with a preposition is something up with which I will not put." By following the rules and creating an obviously stiff sentence, Churchill was, of course, chiding the experts on usage and suggesting that writing is more about making thoughtful choices than about unthinkingly following rules. In any event, when I was considering and reconsidering the sentence, thinking of usage guidelines, and remembering Churchill, I was wearing the mask of the One Who Loves Details. I had slowed way down and spent some time with just one sentence, indeed with just one word. Especially in later stages of revision, putting on this mask is useful.

More Masks

I am running out of room, but pretending I *must* mention one more mask of revision, I will select the *mask of the One Who Likes Surprises*. Whenever the writer wearing this mask sees something predictable, a cliché, a plot development that is certainly believable but not unforeseen, or an ordinary example supporting a claim in an essay, this writer will pounce, revise, and put in something surprising. In my poetry especially, I sometimes cut and paste arbitrarily, just because I feel as if I'm not surprising myself. Now I'll put on the *mask of the One Who Needs to Shut Up,* and I'll "concludify."

So the question is, What *role(s)* do you need to *play* to *perform revision* well? I've discussed only five possible roles here, the fifth one very briefly. You will think of others, other positions to take in relation to what you're writing, for whom, when, and why. And even if you put on one of the five masks mentioned here, you will shape and decorate it, so to speak, according to your own tastes. Revision, in any event, is a performance. There are many ways to play the role of reviser, to produce something wonderful out of the creative tension between what we have already written—an existing draft—and what we hope to write, the better text that the one wearing the mask(s) will bring into being.

Works Cited

Elbow, Peter. 1987. "Closing My Eyes As I Speak: An Argument for Ignoring Audience." *College English* 49 (1): 50–69.

———. 1998. *Writing with Power*. 2d ed. New York: Oxford University Press.

Emigh, John. 1996. *Masked Performance: The Play of Self and Other in Ritual And Theatre*. Philadelphia: University of Pennsylvania Press.

Flower, Linda. 1979. "Writer-Based Prose: A Cognitive Basis for Problems in Writing." *College English* 41 (1): 19–37.

Lavelle, Ellen, and Nancy Zuercher. 1999. "University Students' Beliefs About Writing and Writing Approaches." ERIC Document ED434541. Chicago: University of Illinois. 21 pp.

Four

Revising Research Writing: A Theory and Some Exercises

Alice S. Horning

Writing, like any skill, takes practice. Like playing an instrument and doing scales or playing a sport and doing drills or practicing free throws or point-after kicks, writing requires exercises of various kinds. One part of writing that can be improved through practice is revising. Just as athletes often engage in weight training or aerobic exercise for overall conditioning for all kinds of sports, writers too can engage in activities of various kinds to build their revising muscles. The theory for athletes is that if they are in top overall physical condition, they will excel in their particular sport. A similar theory works for writing. Coaches, trainers, or teachers are particularly helpful, because they can explain aspects of the theory and then guide athletes, musicians, or writers toward developing expertise.

By observing expert writers, I have developed a theory for revising research writing. The exercises in this chapter are drawn from the strategies used by expert writers, based on that theory. No exercise works well or can be sustained if the theory behind it isn't clear, so for each exercise in this chapter, I offer the theory first and then elaborate it to explain the exercises. Two kinds of exercises appear here: guided exercises that provide a first level of practice and then a set of additional strategies for writers to use with their own work.

The Theory

Revision consists of a number of different kinds of activities; together, they produce a smooth, finished text. In my research on revision (as presented in my 2002 book, *Revision Revisited*), I proposed the following definition of *revision* to provide a base for the discussion of how experts work on a text:

> The interaction of conscious and unconscious choices writers make in a draft as they weave readable writing for readers, drawing on a balance of several kinds of self-awareness and on specific skills to provide the finished fabric of a readable text. (5)

This definition allows for revisions that writers make in their minds before, during, and after producing a text as well as the more tangible changes made in a handwritten text or on a computer screen. My goal is to keep the focus on how writers work for readers (their audience) as they revise.

To produce a finished text, my studies show that expert writers rely on *three kinds of awareness* and *four kinds of skills.* I want to explain each of these briefly before describing the guided exercises and strategies you can use to practice and work on your own texts. My research suggests that expert writers understand a great deal about their own behavior as they work on texts and that they make use of a range of skills to prepare their writing for others to read. The writers I studied include not only academic writers but also workplace writers and clergy preparing sermons. All of my research subjects were preparing texts or documents that shared some key features with academic research writing: creating an argument of some kind, drawing on varied types of source materials, addressing a particular audience, and working in a particular genre.

Meta-Rhetorical Awareness

"I always do this . . . then fix it later."

This quote captures the first kind of awareness that expert writers have about themselves, a self-knowledge I have labeled *meta-rhetorical awareness.* Meta-rhetorical awareness means that experts know how to work at writing and the approaches that work for them. Novice writers often don't know their own strategies, since they are usually working on writing in school settings and following teachers' advice. Experienced, professional writers understand their own writing behavior and make conscious choices about how they work on writing. Their ability to do so constitutes their meta-rhetorical awareness.

The writer who provided the quote that opens this section, for example, knew that she started in a way that didn't produce a final text but was a way to begin working; she knew that she needed to go back and make changes after she had created a first draft. The writers I studied for *Revision Revisited* all seemed to understand how they composed, whether their strategies were successful or not. They understood that producing an effective piece of writing entails using techniques that worked and also using techniques that help them produce a text, even if it will need to be rewritten at a later time. They understood the techniques that worked for them. Novice writers, in contrast, often use whatever strategies they have been taught or whatever strategies are required of them, without a clear understanding of which strategies are useful for them as individuals. Developing meta-rhetorical awareness requires observing yourself as you are working and being aware of which strategies seem to work for you.

Revising Exercises for Meta-Rhetorical Awareness

The goal of this exercise is to provide an opportunity for you to work on a brief text and then make observations about your own writing behavior, successful or not. You may want to create a "revision strategy" sheet of advice to yourself about techniques that you find helpful in revising.

Take the following paragraph and make at least three changes in each of these categories: make three additions, three deletions, and three reorderings.

> The weather: everyone complains about it, but no one does anything about it. We complain when it is too hot. We complain when it is too cold. When there is drought, it is a problem for farmers. If there's a flood, people's homes can be damaged. There should be some way to control the weather!

Evaluate the changes and decide whether to keep them or not (Huff 1983). Write a brief paragraph or discuss with other writers how you worked on this task. Where do you feel you succeeded and where did you struggle? What would you do differently if you worked on this text again? Why?

Expert Strategies to Try with Your Own Work

For starting a writing task: Write down a very last sentence for your text. Knowing where you are going to end may be helpful in raising your awareness of where you are taking your reader and the best techniques to help get you there.

For a text already drafted: Read through your text carefully. When you have finished reading, turn over the last page and write down three things you could add (Matsuhashi 1987). Adding to an unseen text may allow you to develop your ideas more fully.

For a text you think you have finished: Think about how you created this piece. Here are a number of prompts that may help you understand the strategies you used to produce the text:

* I tried to make the task my own by . . .
* My personality did or did not affect a choice I made because . . .
* A paragraph where I was especially aware of pace or sentence structure . . .
* The kind of comment I expect/dread/want from readers is . . .
* Discussion of my draft with others caused me to . . .
* Discussion of someone else's draft caused me to . . .
* I tried to use sentence combining/metaphor/organization to . . .
* I broke a rule on purpose to . . .
* I improved my writing efficiency by . . .
* I could improve this in another draft by . . .
* If I could write a completely different paper, I . . .
* Tactics I rejected include . . .
* I went over and over this part until it seemed right to me . . .

These prompts are all jumping-off points for reflection that will help you increase your meta-rhetorical awareness, an awareness of when your approach to writing is effective and when you may need to try something different.

Meta-Strategic Awareness

"I started asking my partner to read my drafts."

This quote comes from one of the attorneys who served as a subject in my study of revision. He had realized, partly from being a subject of research, that he could benefit from sharing his work with another writer. It is not his preferred way of working but is helpful to him on some writing tasks. Expert writers have this kind of awareness, a *meta-strategic awareness*, that allows them to switch to different, nonpreferred strategies when the approaches they usually use don't work or don't work well. Understanding your writing strategies rests in part on understanding your personality, so you may find it helpful to take a personality instrument called the Myers-Briggs Type Indicator. The results of this instrument have been studied extensively in terms of their implications for writing. Developing meta-strategic awareness requires understanding your preferred strategies, knowing when they are working or failing, and being able to switch to other techniques when necessary.

Revising Exercises for Meta-Strategic Awareness

In order to understand your preferences so that you can work differently when the need arises, you can do the following exercises, which may help you understand your preferred strategies (DiTiberio and Jensen 1995, 1–14).

First, try signing your name on a sheet of paper with each hand. Notice the differences in the experience, depending on which hand you use. Most people find writing with their preferred hand easy, so that they feel confident and comfortable. By contrast, signing your name with your other hand is probably awkward, uncomfortable, and not very successful. In a similar way, when you write a paper using preferred strategies, you are likely to feel as though the paper will convey your ideas successfully. However, you will find that using nonpreferred strategies may enable you to be successful in other ways.

A second guided exercise entails thinking consciously about what you like and dislike about writing as a process or activity. Make a list of the features of writing that you enjoy and/or feel are your strengths. Make a second list of processes you feel hinder your ability to convey your ideas. Your goal is to try to focus on the approaches you have used successfully.

Talk with other writers or a teacher or friend about your findings from these exercises.

Expert Strategies to Try with Your Own Work

If your preference for starting a text is to do an outline, try jumping into writing without doing the outline first. If your preference is to jump in, try outlining, mapping, brainstorming, or otherwise planning how you are going to draft the text before you start.

If your preference is to look for facts and details and present those in your writing, rethink your material in terms of the themes or patterns it might have. If your preference is make to your text unique and original, check to see that you have facts to back up your claims and a structure that meets whatever formal requirements you may have been given.

If you prefer to argue with your sources, reshape your writing so that you present the work of others fairly and accurately before you take issue with the content; you may want to include personal examples to strengthen your claims. If you usually try hard to stay connected to your audience and present your values, evaluate and add logical ordering and relationships to the structure of your discussion; state your main points explicitly and briefly; check any writing handbook for a list of transitional words and phrases and try to add several that capture the logical relationships among your ideas.

If you normally stick to the facts and draw conclusions quickly, consider alternative possibilities, contradictions, opposing points of view, using additional sources or material to back up your ideas. If you tend to write at great length, try to condense and make definite, firm points, even though you may not feel as sure of them as your writing suggests (DiTiberio and Jensen 1995, 142–53).

Meta-Linguistic Awareness

"Here's a sentence that really needs some help."

The writer who said this was preparing an academic conference paper and was reading it aloud as part of her work on revision. She had listened to herself read the sentence in question and realized that while it was grammatically correct, it did not read well or sound smooth. Her observations had to do with her knowledge of language and her ability to evaluate the sound of her text, an awareness linguists describe with the phrase *meta-linguistic awareness*. Written language and particularly the language of academic research writing has a particular sound to it. It requires, for example, the use of present tense. Readers expect the writer to introduce and qualify the outside sources being used, usually with some kind of tag phrase like "Ms. X, who has written three books on this topic, notes that . . ." If you are preparing academic writing, you have probably read source materials that refer to others. Pay attention to how the sources are presented in your reading and use those methods as models.

Revising Exercises for Meta-Linguistic Awareness

If you revised the weather paragraph in the guided exercise for meta-rhetorical awareness, read that aloud to yourself now. Try to listen for the overall form of the sentences. See where you say something other than what is written or where you have trouble reading. The sound of the text should point you toward the difficulties that may be there. Alternatively, have someone else read your text (the weather paragraph or another piece) aloud to you. Listen to how it sounds, to where the reader has difficulty rendering the text or says something other than what is written. The difficulties readers have rendering the text aloud can point to language in the text that may need work.

Expert Strategies to Try on Your Own Work

Take another look at the list of transitional words and phrases you consulted while working on meta-strategic awareness (see pages 41–42). See how many of those transitions you use. Could you use more of them or different ones that would capture the relationships among your ideas more effectively?

Read through your text and make a list of words that seem to occur frequently. They will all have something to do with your topic, and their reoccurrence will not be surprising. However, there may be words that you overuse (my own favorite is *important*; others I'm fond of are *particularly* and *especially*). Use a thesaurus or synonym finder to add different words to convey your meaning. Use the search function if you are using a word processor to see if the words you use a lot occur too often.

If you have difficulty finding words that convey your exact meaning, try priming your thinking. You might write in the margin of a paper or in all capital letters within the text onscreen all the words you can think of that are similar in meaning to the one you want. You should then go on to other tasks while your mind works to find the right word. Looking up the synonyms in a thesaurus may give you other ideas but won't necessarily help you find the word you are seeking. Later, you may find that the word you want or need will come to mind.

Developing Collaborative Skills

"I'm not sure I agree with him. . . ."

My expert academic writer had sent a draft of her conference paper to a colleague, also an expert in the field. She asked for substantive, collaborative feedback on the draft from someone quite familiar with her topic. Working collaboratively is a skill that expert writers have. When expert writers collaborate, they hardly ever ask about the thesis, organizational structure, or punctuation. Instead, what they want from colleagues is a substantive response on the *content* of their writing. Novice writers naturally need more help on the basic features of good writing like those just mentioned, but they should also be looking to peer readers for help with the substance of what they are saying. In revising, you will want to ask for help with not only the basic features of your paper but also the more substantive issues.

Revising Exercises for Effective Collaboration

The following series of steps offers a reading strategy that may be helpful to you in working with other students on research papers:

Step 1: Read the introductory paragraph of your peer's paper. Underline the thesis. Write on a separate sheet a one-sentence summary of the gist of the paper. If you cannot find a statement of the point, make note of that. List your expectations of the points the essay will discuss in the margin or on a separate sheet of paper.

Step 2: Read the last paragraph and compare it with the opening for consistency in the point of the paper and for a detailed summary of the points you listed in step 1. Note especially if the statement of the point in the last paragraph seems more clear than the one in the opening. Would the last paragraph make a better opening? Make notes at the end of the paper or on a separate sheet.

Step 3: Read the whole paper, circling any technical errors you see (spelling, punctuation, citation format, etc.). On a separate sheet, make a main-idea outline of the body of the paper. Comment on development, cohesion of argument, and integration of source material in the margins, at the end, or on a separate sheet.

Step 4: List three specific changes you would make if you were revising this paper, and explain why you would make these changes.

Step 5: Check the works cited or references list or bibliography for format and consistency; make notes on the draft if you have questions or doubts.

Step 6: What did you learn from this paper? What questions do you have as a result of reading it? What were your favorite parts? What parts did you find difficult or boring or both? Why? The more you can say to the writer about why you responded as you did, the more helpful you will be.

Expert Strategies to Try with Your Own Work

If you can work with someone else, try reading your paper aloud to this person. Often, as you listen to your text with another person present, you will see and hear things that aren't clear or don't make as much sense as they do inside your head. You can also ask the reader for feedback as you go along, seeing where the reader understands and where the reader gets lost. An alternative strategy is to have another person read your paper to you. Note especially places where the reader has difficulty rendering the written text out loud (if you have a copy, you can mark this as the reader moves along; writing researchers call this *miscue analysis*). When a reader stumbles in the oral rendition of a text, it may signal difficulties with understanding. Although readers may deviate from a written text for other reasons, often a different response than what is on the page is a signal that the writer hasn't been clear or hasn't written what the reader expected to find. (The reading-aloud strategy is discussed in detail by Meredith Sue Willis in *Deep Revision* 1993, 75–76; for a discussion of the implications of oral renderings of a text that differ from the printed version, see Kenneth Goodman 1965).

You may also want to try to find an expert on your topic. This expert might be a university faculty member, a colleague at work, or a friend, relative, or other person who knows something about your topic. One of my experts writes medical texts but is not a doctor and has no formal training in science. His writing is reviewed thoroughly by several medical experts and he always makes the content changes they recommend. If possible, you may want to follow his example, getting substantive help with your text.

Developing Skills with Genre

"I've got this format in my word processor at work; I'll just re-create it here in order to set up this draft."

The writer who produced this quote was preparing to work on the transformation of previously published material to a different genre for a new publication. To revise the material, he needed to format it in a style consistent with the new book, hence the need to set up the new format. Academic research writing is a highly specialized genre but only one of many, such as news reports, procedural manuals, encyclopedia entries, business letters, and memos. Expert writers understand the differences in genres and have the skill to move flexibly from one genre to another. A genre usually has easily recognizable features. For example, almost everyone knows the genre of dictionary entries; this genre serves as the basis for the game Balderdash.

Revision Exercise to Develop Skills with Genre

To practice switching between two different genres, take the following well-known poem by Lewis Carroll, "Jabberwocky" (1960, 448), and rewrite it briefly as a news story or research report. Share your version with other writers if you are working in a class or a group.

'Twas brillig, and the slithy toves
    Did gyre and gimble in the wabe:
All mimsy were the borogoves,
    And the mome raths outgrabe.

"Beware the Jabberwock, my son!
    The jaws that bite, the claws that catch!
Beware the Jujub bird, and shun
    The frumious Bandersnatch!"

He took his vorpal sword in hand;
    Long time the manxome foe he sought—
So rested he by the Tumtum tree,
    And stood awhile in thought.

And, as in uffish thought he stood,
    The Jabberwock, with eyes of flame,
Came whiffling through the tulgey wood,
    And burbled as it came!

One, two! One, two! And through and through
    The vorpal blade went snicker-snack!
He left it dead, and with its head
    He went galumphing back.

"And hast thou slain the Jabberwock?
    Come to my arms, my beamish boy!
O frabjous day! Callooh, Callay!"
    He chortled in his joy.

'Twas brillig, and the slithy toves
    Did gyre and gimble in the wabe:
All mimsy were the borogroves,
    And the mome raths outgrabe.

Expert Strategies to Try with Your Own Work

Take a text you are working on and reduce it to a summary of one hundred or two hundred words (good advice for how to do this appears in the *APA Style Manual*). Alternatively, turn your entire text into a PowerPoint presentation. Could you write a news report based on the information you have from your research? If you were going to create a webpage based on your findings and main idea, what would you put on the page in addition to the text, and why? What colors, sounds, images, and layout would you use? How does thinking about alternative formats change your view of your text?

Developing Skills with Text and Context

"I'm thinking about five people I know well."
    The writer who said this was a member of the clergy preparing a sermon. She had been taught to think about her audience in terms of five members of her congregation who were representative of the congregation as a whole. Expert writers use this approach to thinking about what Bitzer called the "rhetorical situation," including an awareness of audience, topic, purpose, and the need for the particular piece of writing being produced (Bitzer 1983). My expert writer used her skills with text and context to think about the biblical text she was discussing and how her listeners would react to it as well as to her message. Good writers are aware of both how their texts work in the real world situation in which they occur and how the texts they have chosen to include within their writing help illustrate their ideas. They use a variety of

techniques to address issues of text and context; they draw on outside sources in very specific ways to support their own points.

Revising Exercise for Skills with Text and Context

Here is a structured way of thinking about your writing situation from the work of anthropologist Dell Hymes (1972) for thinking about text and context and developing skills in analyzing the context in which you are writing along with the texts you are using to support your ideas. The following series of questions may help you think about the text and context of your research project:

1. What is the setting and scene for your text?
2. Who are the participants?
3. What is the goal you hope to achieve with your report/paper?
4. What sequence are you using to present your ideas? Why?
5. What tone have you adopted, formal, informal, or otherwise? Is this the best and most appropriate tone for this piece?
6. What mode of delivery will you use for your text (standard written research paper, webpage, oral report, all three)?
7. Which conventions apply to the kind of text you are presenting? Have you observed these conventions?
8. What genre of text are you writing? How does the genre affect what you say and how you say it?

Discuss your responses to each of these questions with other writers working on similar tasks or with your teacher.

Expert Strategies to Try with Your Own Work

You can use the questions from the previous section on any text you might be preparing. If you are working alone, try writing out your answers to these questions informally; doing so will help you think about the text and context in which you are working.

Alternatively, turn your text into a different type of text, such as a letter to a particular person, such as your legislator, your mom, or your significant other. How does changing the audience influence what you say and how you say it? Imagine your own audience of five people you know well. How does *this* audience affect what you say and how you say it?

Developing Revision Skills

"Let me check this in the stylebook."

The writer who said this is someone who has edited an academic journal for many years, and yet even he found himself referring to a style manual to check a particular formatting issue. Expert writers make use of many tools in their work, both print and electronic. Dictionaries, thesauruses, grammar and mechanics handbooks, style guides for citation of sources and other text preparation requirements (such as the *Modern Language Association Style Manual* [MLA] or the *American Psychological Association Style Manual* [APA]) are all commonly found on the shelves of professional writers. They also rely on spellcheckers, grammar checkers, and other features of today's highly sophisticated word processors. These are simply the tools of the writer's trade, available for use by any writer. To use the tools of revision effectively, it is helpful to know your own strengths and weaknesses as a writer, so you know what to look for and what resources are available to help you do so.

Revising Exercise with Revision Tools

If you are working in a writing class or have prior papers that have been corrected by a writing teacher, you can develop your skill with revision by knowing what kinds of problems tend to turn up in your writing. Start making a list of the technical weaknesses that have appeared in your papers. If you write by hand and make many spelling errors, start a list of those. Do the same thing with run-ons, fragments, mechanics errors, and the like. Try to get a database of at least ten errors in each of your major problem areas (twenty-five is better for spelling problems). Try to find a pattern to the errors. If you know the categories into which the errors fall, you may want to talk with your teacher or another writer or a trained writing tutor about the specific kinds of errors you make in order to understand the logic behind them (this strategy is based on the work of Shaughnessy 1977).

Research shows that you are probably making similar kinds of errors as a result of some confusion about a basic rule or a lack of knowledge of rules (for using apostrophes or coordinating conjunctions or the like). You may find some practice sentences in a grammar handbook of use, along with study of the rules or principles. If you understand where your problems lie, you can make a list of points to check in revision. A teacher or tutor can help you with this project and may also be able to direct you to useful tools for addressing your problems in books or at key websites.

Expert Strategies to Try with Your Own Work

If you know where your weaknesses are, you will be able to develop strategies for using revision tools to address them. You may have use for the grammar checker and spellchecker on your word processor, though these won't solve all your problems. You may also want to acquire or get access (in a physical or virtual library) to standard reference books: a dictionary, a thesaurus, an almanac, and an encyclopedia. You should find out about the standard style manual for your academic area and get a copy of the latest edition.

Some other techniques to try include using cut and paste in your word processor to reverse your opening and ending paragraphs in a paper to see if your ending could work effectively as a starting point for your paper. Another tool used by experts is to let a draft cool for a day, a week, or a month if time allows and then go back and look at it again with fresh eyes (Willis 1993).

Expert writers use the tools of the writer's trade all the time. They don't know all the rules and requirements, but they know where and how to look up whatever information they need to produce good writing. Though many of the tools address the details of writing and details may simply not be your strength or preference, you can get writing right without much effort through the effective use of revision tools.

Moving On

Like other skills, writing takes time and practice to develop. Like other skills, writing requires some fundamentals that can be learned and practiced and may or may not apply to a particular task. Just as playing the scales does not always apply directly to playing songs or symphonies, practicing revision will not always apply to every piece of writing you produce. You probably won't use any of the strategies you've practiced here when you send email to your friends or write thank-you notes to Grandma. However, when you engage in academic, professional, or other kinds of research-based writing, the exercises here should help you develop useful awarenesses and skills you can apply to your revision process.

Works Cited

American Psychology Association. 1994. *Publication Manual of the American Psychological Association.* Washington, D.C.: American Psychological Association.

Bitzer, L. 1983. "The Rhetorical Situation." In *The Rhetoric of Western Thought*, 3d ed., ed. J. L. Golden, G. F. Berquist, and W. E. Coleman. Dubuque, IA: Kendall-Hunt. (Original work published 1968.) 17–24.

Carroll, Lewis. 1960. "Jabberwocky." In *Immortal Poems of the English Language*, ed. Oscar Williams. New York: Washington Square. 448.

DiTiberio, John, and George Jensen. 1995. *Writing and Personality: Finding Your Voice, Your Style, Your Way.* Palo Alto, CA: Davies-Black.

Goodman, Kenneth S. 1965. "A Linguistic Study of Cues and Miscues in Reading." In *Elemental English* 42: 639–43.

Horning, Alice S. 2002. *Revision Revisited.* Cresskill, NJ: Hampton.

Huff, R.K. 1983. "Teaching Revision: A Model of the Drafting Process." *College English* 45: 800–16.

Hymes, Dell. 1972. "Models of the Interaction of Language and Social Life." In *Directions in Sociolinguistics: The Ethnography of Communication*, ed. J. J. Gumperz and Dell Hymes. New York: Holt. 35–71.

Matsuhashi, Ann. 1987. "Revising the Plan and Altering the Text." In *Writing in Real Time: Modeling Production Processes*, ed. Ann Matsuhashi. Norwood, NJ: Ablex. 197–223.

Shaughnessy, Mina. 1977. *Errors and Expectations: A Guide for the Teacher of Basic Writing*. New York: Oxford University Press.

Willis, Meredith Sue. 1993. *Deep Revision*. New York: Teachers and Writers Collaborative.

Five

From Correct to Effect: Revising Alternate Styles

Melissa A. Goldthwaite

Recently, a business major signed up for my creative nonfiction course; his advisor had suggested the class to fulfill a humanities requirement. Neither the student nor his advisor had any idea it was a writing course. One afternoon after class, this student expressed nervousness about participating ("I don't know what all those words like *tone* and *syntax* mean"), about his writing ("Is it any good?"), and about his grade ("Do you think I can get a B?"). We talked about the course and his work, and then I asked, "Even though you didn't know what you were getting in to, do you feel OK about being in the class?"

"Yeah, it's great," he said. "You let us do all the things my other teachers say are wrong."

I was a little taken aback, though somewhat pleased that his enthusiasm balanced his nervousness. As many writers know, it's sometimes OK to do what you've been taught to see as incorrect: use the first person in essays, purposely include fragments or one-sentence paragraphs for emphasis, begin a sentence with a conjunction as a transition technique, use contractions and even slang when developing a conversational tone, play with repetition, create long sentences (the kinds computer grammar checkers always flag), and write in sections, using white space to guide the reader. Sometimes, it's more helpful to consider conventions of writing rather than correctness. It all depends on the form you're writing, your purpose, your audience, and the effect you're going for.

It's important for writers of all kinds to examine and use a range of strategies, including those that constitute what Winston Weathers refers to as "alternate style," elements of *style*—such as repetition, fragments, long sentences, lists, more than one voice, and wordplay—that professional writers use every day.

At the same time, however, not everything goes. Alternate styles need to be used as carefully and as knowledgeably as more traditional grammars of style. Every draft can use work. That is, every writer needs to revise, to rethink the very structures of whole essays, paragraphs, and sentences. Every decision, every pause, every word counts.

If it is true, as the business student observed, that I allow—even ask— the writers I work with to do much of what their other teachers say is wrong in their writing, if I question the rules fundamental to their previous training, what standards guide their revision? Writers do need to know the conventions of the genres they write, and handbooks can be one starting place for revision, but revising alternate styles ultimately requires moving away from the safety of books that outline what is correct and incorrect. It requires knowing which conventions to break, when to break them, and which ones to remake anew. It requires knowing yourself as a writer, finding readers you can trust, and learning to translate responses to your writing into opportunities for revision.

Becoming Your Own Audience

Knowing yourself as a writer—determining your own stylistic strengths and weaknesses—means becoming an audience for your own work, seeing your work as worthy of time and attention. Whether you write to express yourself or to answer an assignment, if anyone else will be reading your work, you'll most likely need to do some revision in order to communicate more effectively. Many times, your friends, teachers, and classmates will offer suggestions for revision (more on that shortly), but even before you hand your writing over to someone else, you can learn to become your own best reader.

Becoming your own audience requires balancing the demands of being both writer and receiver, seeing yourself as occupying these two different roles simultaneously. Instead of asking yourself, Did I say what I wanted to say? you'll need to ask questions that help you look outward: What's the effect of the choices I've made? Will the form I've chosen communicate what I want my readers to understand? Will it allow them to experience vicariously what I've experienced?

This experience can be emotional, physical, or intellectual (or some mix of all three). The form and style you use can help you communicate the excitement of research and discovery, the power of an emotional state, the feeling of a physical state, or the satisfaction of newly acquired knowledge. For example, at the end of the section "Hell," in her mixed-genre memoir *Leap*, Terry Tempest Williams (2000) uses several elements of alternate style to create a sensation of brokenness. She leaves out punctuation and spaces between words and emphasizes her point through repetition; she writes on page 126:

> Whataboutheconvenantswehavemadenottobebrokenwearebrokenweare
> brokenthisrecordofoursisbrokenisbrokenisbrokenwearebrokenthisrecordofours

Because Williams uses no end punctuation to bring the repetition to a close, readers get the sense of continued brokenness: the sentence is broken in a conventional sense. It's not "correct," but it certainly communicates. Each time you make choices between alternate styles and conventional style in your own writing and revision, ask yourself *what* and *how* that choice communicates to others.

Every choice communicates something, and there will be times when your choices say something that you don't wish to say. Or if you say the same thing again and again through your choice of form and style, readers may get bored or confused. Sometimes, you need to curb your own tendencies. And since you're probably the person most familiar with your work, you're often the best judge of what you need to work on.

I love long sentences—lists, embedded clauses, parenthetical qualifications and illustrations, repetition, parallel structures, dashes—the winding sentence, the rising and falling sentence, the sentence that seems to have and live a life of its own. As a writer, I'm naturally inclined toward the labyrinthine sentence, that "long complex sentence, with a certain 'endless' quality to it, full of convolutions, marked by appositives, parentheses, digressions" (Weathers 1980, 16). But sometimes, I lose readers. And so for every 36-word sentence (or 136 words), I know I need to consider a 3-word sentence. Or an 18-word sentence, or maybe 12 words: small, medium, large. Balance.

Knowing my tendency toward long sentences, when I revise, I've learned a strategy: I read my work aloud. If I stumble or get lost in my own sentences, I know I have to change something: sometimes the punctuation, other times the structure or length of the sentence. There's nothing wrong with long sentences; in fact, often they're quite effective, but I know that readers need guides through the labyrinths—and that there can't be too many turns or my readers will get frustrated.

To help other writers consider their own tendencies, I provide a list of "if . . . then" revision exercises. Here are a few examples from that list:

- If you have a section of dialogue in your essay and you're simply reporting what was said, add actions to show what the speakers were doing while they were speaking. Or add a description of the surroundings to help readers visualize the scene.

- If you've included more than four fragments in your essay, write a labyrinthine sentence—make it at least eighty-six words. Include a list. (For example, see Andrea Bucci's writing on page 58.)

- If you want to emphasize something in your essay, use a fragment, use repetition, or use a one-sentence paragraph.

- If you've written your essay in sections and are not satisfied with the order, reorganize (by cutting and pasting in your word processor—and remember to keep the original in case you discover through this process that the original sequence really does work best). Try at least two of these options: chronological order; reverse chronological order, with flashbacks and flash-forwards; from distant to personal; from personal to more general/universal.

- If you tend to write long paragraphs, revise your essay to include the following: two one-sentence paragraphs, one three-sentence paragraph, and three two-sentence paragraphs.

- If you've written your essay in sections, take one section out (the one you think is weakest) and write a new section in its place.

When I gave a longer version of this list to my creative nonfiction students, one writer, Kristin Ryan, realized that she tends toward long paragraphs. Not overly long—in fact, her paragraphs are probably standard length, averaging twelve sentences. She packs a lot of information into each paragraph. She recognized this tendency, and in revision, Kristin broke up a twelve-sentence paragraph into six shorter ones, creating emphasis in recounting an exchange she and her dad had about where she should go for a study-abroad trip. Here are just the first few sentences of Kristin's paragraph and her revision:

Original:

But Dad wanted me to go to Ireland. "You have family there who could take care of you. And it's much closer and safer." Sure, Dad. Let's pick a place where we have connections, like we always do. Why take chances in life? Play it safe and try not to wonder what could happen. I don't think so!

Revision:

But Dad wanted me to go to Ireland.
    "You have family there who could take care of you. And it's much closer and safer."
    Sure, Dad. Let's pick a place where we have connections, like we always do. Why take chances in life? Play it safe and try not to wonder what could happen.
    I don't think so!

In this revision, the words remain the same, but by breaking up one longer paragraph into several shorter ones, Kristin is able to emphasize not only her father's position but also her response to what he was saying. She accentuates contrasts. Using white space on the page—through paragraph breaks or section breaks—creates a pause for readers, allowing them time (even a just a split second) to take in what you're trying to get across.

It's important to recognize your own tendencies, your favored forms, phrases, and constructions. These tendencies are, in part, what make your writing style your own. But they are also helpful guides to revision, to becoming a better, more flexible writer.

In "Responding to, Evaluating, and Grading Alternate Style," Wendy Bishop offers several questions writers can ask themselves as they consider their own writing:

- Can I describe why this writing requires this style/format?

- Are there places in the writing where I covered up, patched, ignored problems I was having understanding my own writing goals or aims?

- If I recast this as a traditionally styled writing, what would I lose and what would I gain?
- In my final draft, am I paying attention to the reader? Have I done everything I can to "teach" the reader how to read my piece while still maintaining the integrity of my writing goals and ideas? (1997, 175)

Asking yourself questions, such as the ones Bishop offers, will encourage you to think about your own intentions in writing and revising, and they will also help you begin to imagine some of the effects of the form and style you've chosen, effects that will become even more evident when you give your writing to others and they share their responses.

Listening to the Responses of Others

Many times, you'll be able to recognize the strengths and weaknesses of your writing on your own, but there will also be times when listening to others will provide the guidance for revision you need. Writing teachers use small-group work, discussions of published writing, peer response, individual conferences, and whole-class workshops because they know that as hard as we try to be an audience for our own work, we still need the responses of others. We need to listen to those writers whose experiences differ from our own, those who have read different books, those whose stylistic tendencies—because they differ from ours—remind us of a full range of options.

There are times when group consensus leads us to make certain choices in revision. For example, Andrea Bucci, an education major, wrote a segmented essay made up of numerous "crots" (Weathers' term for bits of text, often short sections in a longer piece). Already a strong essay, there was nothing wrong with any of the sections; they all fit her overall focus on the relationship between teaching and learning. When we workshopped Andrea's essay in class, though, several classmates pointed to one section as less effective than the others.

Andrea listened closely as readers praised the sections that included vivid detail and reflection based on personal experience. In the workshop, it became apparent that many had a harder time seeing the relevance of her section on the Walt Disney Corporation's Outstanding Teacher of the Year award winner. In a way, the section was relevant since it detailed the philosophy and practice of an outstanding teacher, whose philosophy of teaching was similar to Andrea's, but it didn't have the same energy that the sections informed by Andrea's own teaching and learning experience did. So in revision, she took the Outstanding Teacher of the Year section out and replaced it with a section on another outstanding teacher, the professor who inspired Andrea to become a teacher herself. This important revision resulted from being attentive to the responses of others.

More often, however, there won't be group consensus—especially when you're working with alternate styles. What strikes some readers as quirky in a fun and interesting way might strike other readers as odd in a distracting way. As the writer, you're left to weigh the responses. In another essay, a student recounted a conversation he'd had with an acquaintance at a party. In the essay, the acquaintance calls him "Dood." When we workshopped the essay, some readers thought *Dood* was a typo, while others interpreted it as reflective of the character who used the word in conversation. In revision, the writer was left with the task of considering not only his own intention (was it a typo or intentional?) but also the effect it had on others (for some, it took away from the integrity of the piece; for others, it added to it).

There's a history of language variegation in alternately styled writing, "a pressing against the walls of ordinary/orthodox vocabulary, a playing with words/word forms to achieve a special kind of lexical texture—a reading surface that is exciting and rebellious all at once" (Weathers 1980, 30). This writer had several choices to make in revision: he could change *Dood* to *Dude* (its conventional spelling), leave it as he'd written it, or add more language variegation to his essay, especially in the dialogue with the acquaintance at the party. This third choice would show that the "misspellings" were elements of character development, not simple mistakes. As this example illustrates, sometimes, you don't have to make an either/or choice, accepting one reader's suggestion and ignoring another's. You can listen closely to the responses of others and use their comments as compasses—direction for revision.

The previous two examples of listening to the responses of others assume that you have access to a group of careful readers. If you're taking a writing class, you probably do have such a group, but if you don't (or if you won't when your class has ended), you can still seek out readers. Some colleges and communities have established writing groups that you can join—or you can create your own. The key is to find readers, even just two or three, who will ask you the hard questions, the ones that will help you think more deeply and carefully about your own writing. Look for those readers who will tell you how they read your text: where they were interested, where they got confused, where they were delighted or moved. Look for those who will ask about your purpose and help you better achieve that purpose through revision. Look for those whose work you can read and respond to as well, for reading, writing, and response are reciprocal activities.

More or Less Alternate Style

OK. So you're willing to consider the strengths and weaknesses of your own work and you have a group of readers who can help, but you still need some specific strategies for revising alternate styles—especially since you're used to following the rules when you revise. I've already suggested that your writing handbook won't necessarily help, but maybe it will. Don't throw it away; just start trying to figure out when and how it's useful.

In *An Alternate Style*, Weathers points to the value of "having access to 'both sides of the coin'"; he argues that

> the "contrary" or "alternate" completes a picture, saves us from the absolute-
> ness of one single style, provides us with the stimulating, illuminating, and
> refreshing *opposite* that makes the traditional grammar of style even more
> meaningful and useful: as the alternate grammar of style more and more
> takes on strong and viable identity, so the traditional style is lifted from the
> lethargy/monotony of its solitude. (1980, 11–12)

This focus on both sides of the coin allows writers—especially those in the process of revising—to see the importance of strategies of both Grammar A (traditional grammars of style found in handbooks) and Grammar B (alternate styles).

In revising alternate styles, you have numerous options: you can make what's alternate more traditional or make your writing even more experimental to suit your purposes. The key to revising alternate styles is not to be a slave to the demands of either Grammar A or Grammar B, but to weigh the effect of each stylistic choice you make.

Rules are often worth breaking. One of Weathers' rules, for example, is that a "writer commits herself to one grammar of style or the other early in a composition, and once she has asked her reader to accept one style or the other, she must not 'switch'" (1980, 39–40). Writers of both Grammar A and Grammar B know, however, that these grammars depend on each other, that many pieces of writing are neither fully alternately styled nor fully traditional.

Depending on context and audience, you may have more or less freedom to take chances, to be playful in your writing. If you're writing a formal analysis paper for a history class, you may not want to fill it with labyrinthine sentences or fragments, but you may find yourself using language variegation in the title or in the first line to grab your reader's attention. Many readers like to be surprised—as long as they know the writer intended the surprise through a thoughtful use of language (rather than through typos or other mistakes).

Likewise, if you're writing an alternately styled text, the rules of traditional grammar can guide your revision. Perhaps you're writing a segmented essay (what Weathers refers to as a "collage" or "montage"), a piece made up of multiple crots or sections, and one of those crots is a labyrinthine sentence. Use of a parallel structure and traditional punctuation might help guide your reader through the labyrinth.

Here are some additional options, some rules for breaking and remaking, as you revise your alternately styled texts:

1. Use traditional grammar and punctuation in labyrinthine sentences—and embed one in an essay made up of otherwise traditional sentences.

Weathers states, "Usually, if traditional sentence types are to be mixed with the more radical forms, the mix will involve only traditional types and sentence fragments. Rarely do the traditional sentences and labyrinthine sentence mix successfully" (1980, 16). In this statement, Weathers offers some general guidance; he uses terms such as *usually* and *rarely*. Your task is to find an exception to this rule, to mix traditional and labyrinthine sentences successfully.

Andrea Bucci did just this in revising her essay "Chalk Talk." For an essay made up of otherwise traditional sentences, she wrote the following labyrinthine sentence, showing that alternate styles can be used even in a largely traditional form, a teaching philosophy:

> I don't think I ever realized how arbitrary the education of educators is; all we are equipped with is Pavlov's dog, Skinner's white mice, Bloom's taxonomy of higher order thinking, lesson plan formats, diversity statistics, lessons on morphology, phonology, semantics and syntax, the ideas of Dewey, the format of an IEP, or IFSP, an adaptation, the definition of ADD, ADHD, ODD and the IDEA law; how does it all help us when we need to be learning the practical aspects of teaching, such as dealing with board meetings, angry parents, the blame game, grading and rubrics, public speaking, class control, patience, frustration and anger; how are we being educated to educate when I am a senior and feel unequipped and unprepared to enter a real life classroom?

The seemingly endless quality of this sentence communicates the writer's anxiety about her upcoming student teaching. Through lists, it shows the breadth of knowledge she has—and the practical experience she simultaneously desires and fears.

2. Make a double-voiced text a triple- or quadruple-voiced text.

Perhaps you've done some collaborative writing and have a text with alternating sections, some written by you, others written by your collaborator. What would happen if you added another voice, another perspective, to the mix? Your revision would probably require more than a simple addition; you and your initial collaborator would likely need to revise in response to the newer perspective.

In making a double-voiced text a triple- or quadruple-voiced text, the voices don't need to be representative of different people. As Weathers explains, "Writers use double-voice many times when they feel that they could say this *or* that about a subject; when they feel that two attitudes toward a subject are equally valid; when they wish to suggest that there are two sides to the story" (1980, 24). All of those voices might be part of you—and there may be more than two. Perhaps you have an essay that, in one part, narrates a childhood experience from the perspective of the child (how you experienced the situation when you were five) and then, in another section, looks back on the situation from an adult perspective—your perspective at eighteen or twenty. What would happen if you added another section: this one from the remembered perspective of being ten or the imagined perspective of looking back on the situation when you're fifty-two? Your text, then, goes beyond the bounds of double voice; it becomes polyvocal. As you incorporate additional voices, though, be sure to pay attention to form, so your readers know what's going on. Multiple voices can be invigorating, but if they're not presented clearly, they can also be confusing.

3. Order your lists.

Weathers observes that the sequence of lists in pieces that use alternate-style strategies "is generally arbitrary and meaningless" (1980, 20). In most cases, I agree with him. There can be something wonderfully surprising about a list in which there is little or no discernable order, but order can also be an artful principle, especially when the order isn't blatant. Perhaps you've listed the ingredients in a fruit salad in whatever order they came to mind. Now find an order for the list, but resist the urge to make it an expected order. Readers might expect you to list the ingredients in the order they should be used—like a recipe—but a fruit salad allows for variation in order: strawberries, mandarin oranges, banana, white grapes, blueberries, plums. Many readers won't notice that I've listed these fruits in the order of their color, making a rainbow of this salad; this detail, to some, might seem irrelevant, but attention to details makes writing, reading, and revising more pleasurable.

4. Transition between crots, but do it subtly.

Of the crot, Weathers writes: "It is fundamentally an autonomous unit, characterized by the absence of any transitional devices that might relate it to the preceding or subsequent crots" (1980, 14). There are times, however, when readers benefit from transitions, some way of linking the sections or getting a sense of your overall structure. Marisa Fulton did just this in revising an essay she wrote on her experience of living for a summer in New York. While in her earlier draft each section was, indeed, autonomous, in revision she transitioned gracefully between sections. She moved, for example, from a section on confronting class and cultural differences with her colleagues to a section on the reality of living on a budget.

In Marisa's first draft, her section "Jewish" moved from a coworker recounting what Sarah Jessica Parker wore to her sister's wedding to a section titled "$175 a Week," which opened, "That's what I live on a week: $175." In revision, the movement looked like this:

> "Did I tell you that Sarah Jessica Parker came to my sister Hannah's wedding? Of course it was way before *Sex and the City* was popular. Yeah, she is an old family friend from my mother's side. Listen to what she was wearing—a long, balck Dolce dress and . . ."
>
> $175 a week
>
> There is definitely no money for me to buy a Dolce and Gabbana dress like Sarah Jessica's for thousands of dollars. I live on just $175 a week, deposited by my father on Saturday, ready for withdrawal bright and early Monday at the ATM in the lobby of News Corp.

Though both versions work, the revised version highlights the associational nature of essay writing, making the writer's private associations even more clear to readers.

5. *Think about a rule you followed in writing the draft you're now revising, a rule you wanted to break but didn't. Break that rule now. Or make up a new rule and follow it. Try something you've always wanted to try.*

Elsie Rogers, in "Stretch a Little and Get Limber," writes that "by playing with form, style, and constantly changing the rules . . . we learn how to use the rules to our advantage and how to make up our own rules when necessary" (1997, 25). If there are a lot of rules you've wanted to break and create anew, formulate your own Grammar C and revise accordingly. See what works and doesn't; learn from your mistakes. It's your turn to provide the example now.

Like the business major who learned a new grammar of style in his first creative writing class and learned, too, to see the value of the traditional grammar he already knew, I hope you will see rules—either the rules of traditional grammar or the rules of alternate style—as a large wardrobe rather than as straightjackets. Go for texture, color, the right fit. Try all your options on in your writing; mix and match; take stock of the appearance of your text, knowing you can change; ask advice from others (How does this look? What do you think?); and give yourself time and space to play—and to revise.

Works Cited

Bishop, Wendy, ed. 1997. *Elements of Alternate Style: Essays on Writing and Revision.* Portsmouth, NH: Boynton/Cook.

Rogers, Elsie. 1997. "Stretch a Little and Get Limber: Warming up to (and with) Grammar B." In *Elements of Alternate Style: Essays on Writing and Revision,* ed. Wendy Bishop, 19–25. Portsmouth, NH: Boynton/Cook.

Weathers, Winston. 1980. *An Alternate Style: Options in Composition.* Rochelle Park, NJ: Hayden.

Williams, Terry Tempest. 2000. *Leap.* New York: Pantheon.

Six

Subterranean Rulesick Blues

Maggie Gerrity

> Although the masters make the rules
> For the wise men and the fools
> I got nothing, Ma, to live up to.
> —Bob Dylan, "It's Alright, Ma"

I grew up with rules that were absolute: believe this, say this, sing that, don't question, repeat after me—because I said so, because I'm your mother, because this is what everyone else believes, because it's the word of God, hallelujah, forever and ever, amen. My father is a prison warden and my mother a district attorney's secretary; I always equated breaking the rules with loss of freedom and harsh punishments. And if that weren't bad enough, when I wore the stiff button-down shirts and scratchy gray skirts of a Catholic high school, I came to believe even the slightest mistakes might mean eternal damnation.

How can I not be a little ambivalent about rules?

As a teenager, I plastered my walls with posters and magazine cutouts of rock stars, men my mother glared at every time she came into my room to yell at me to turn the music down and get started on my algebra homework. Music was the escape I so desperately needed. *Achtung Baby* and *August and Everything After* couldn't dissolve the dead-end steel town of my childhood, but sometimes with the headphones on and the volume up, it almost seemed like they could.

U2 lead singer Bono, in his leather pants and oversized black fly goggles, became my savior—a blue-eyed, earringed genius songwriter, the smoking, drinking sort of troublemaker about whom my mother had always warned me. My rebellion continued: I bought Everclear's *Sparkle and Fade*, the first CD I'd ever had to feature the F-word. I played the songs containing it over and over after school, testing the word for whenever I could brandish it beyond the sky blue walls of my bedroom.

These days, my rock star idols seem tame at best. Eminem shouts more obscenities in one song than Everclear does on a whole album. Bono is settling into middle age, thinking he's a modern-day Jesus who can save the world one

South African at a time; he's even been nominated for the Nobel Peace Prize. Tickets for U2's last tour would've cost me more than a hundred dollars.

Now that I no longer live with my parents, a new revolt no longer seems worth the effort; I drop in for holidays, maybe other occasional visits, and I'm never going to change their minds. Instead, now I blast music from *their* generation: Janis Joplin's "Piece of My Heart" and Dylan's "Subterranean Homesick Blues"; the Beatles in their drug-induced psychedelic years; Mick Jagger defiantly sexual in "Honky Tonk Women" and "Brown Sugar"; the Dead; James Taylor; Joni Mitchell. During a recent trip back to Pennsylvania, my mother paused one day in my doorway, cocked her head, and asked me to turn it *up*. I took it as a victory, however small.

My ambivalence about rules has not left me now that I've become a writer. Of course I fancy myself one day joining the canon alongside writers whose work makes me marvel—Hemingway, Virginia Woolf, Tim O'Brien— and in order to do that, I know I must follow certain conventions that will allow my work to be understood. At the same time, though, I want my writing to have the feel of my music collection. I want it to have the serenity of James Taylor and the swagger of Bono. I revise and edit following the rules—of standard written English, of grammar, of the style of the magazines and journals in which I hope to be published. But being a writer also means constantly revising on a higher level, too—changing as a person, watching my understanding of the craft and of myself constantly evolve and become more complicated. Even now, writing this essay, I find myself revising the way I feel about revising and about the role of rules in my writing and in my life.

Sometimes, I'll admit, I need rules to anchor me, to give me a box into which I can pack whatever mess I want to write about. Early drafts spill onto the page, going in four different directions; half the time, they barely make sense to *me*, let alone to a teacher or fellow workshop member. Revision enables me both to discover the truth hidden in that mess on the page and to deliver that truth in a way that will allow my readers to walk beside me instead of chasing after me for clues.

This was especially the case during a poetry workshop I took in college. For several years I'd been trying to find a way to face my biggest demon, the loss of a close friend and beloved teacher to AIDS. Prose gave me too much room to wander, to ramble, to ache and grieve all over again. Sonnets, fourteen-line poems with a regular number of syllables per line and a rhyme scheme, enabled me to deal with small, representative moments—the calculus exam I took two days after his funeral, my first visit to his grave—and I felt safe knowing that after 140 syllables, I could stop. I could take a deep breath, go downstairs for a glass of milk or a game of gin rummy with my roommates. I gave myself permission to walk away, at least temporarily. I know I will write about this subject matter much more in my career. Even now, seven years later, there are parts of it I still don't feel ready to approach.

The series, titled "Last Rites," was a huge breakthrough for me, both in my growth as a writer and in my ability to face this cataclysmic event. Instead of forcing every detail onto the page, I allowed myself to write a very exploratory rough draft. I will revise this story for the rest of my life, using this last section as a starting point:

> I always get
> the last-minute assignments—
> meetings, disasters—& though I meant
>
> to ask for the afternoon off I got
> stuck with another, as if they forgot
>
> I'm part-time. Sophomore health class, CCHS,
> an alum with HIV
> wants to share his mess-
>
> age, & I take notes from the back.
> Imagine my surprise when he asks,
>
> "How many of you
> have lost someone to AIDS?"
> Some freeze, others fidget or rearrange
>
> their notebooks, uncomfortable at the thought.
> . . . *the Word was with God, & the Word was God* . . .
>
> I raise my hand. (This is off the record.)
> No. Write this down.
> Every single word.

Notice that I don't stick to form absolutely. I chose to break some of the lines to indicate how the subject matter wanted to spill out of the confines of the poem. But without the sonnet's form, its limitations, I never would've been able to tackle this subject.

I don't always feel this protected by conventions, though. In a nonfiction workshop last summer, I found that I couldn't address my feelings about how I secretly felt about a good friend. Every time I got close enough to evoke a scene, I froze up. I wanted to be objective, to pull away from myself without having to fictionalize anything. By changing the point of view from first to second, I could be both character and narrator; Maggie the writer could find meaning in events that baffled Maggie drunk on kamikazes and too much Rolling Rock. After four drafts, the essay, titled "Kamikazes," turned out exactly as I'd hoped it would. I revisited an emotionally tense scene without flinching because I backed away and observed it objectively. This passage comes from the most climactic part of the piece:

> But when he pulls you into a good night hug in the dining room, you will blurt out that you love him, that you've needed him to know for months but never knew how to say it. He will not get angry, as you expect, will not ask why you've kept the truth from him all these months. He will not say *I'm gay*, a confession you've been trying to prepare yourself for, something neither of

you seems quite willing to believe. He'll already have given you a T-shirt to
sleep in, and you'll be wearing it and thinking how perfectly it fits, how soft
it is. He will not do what he always does, change the subject or offer you a
glass of water or walk into another room. He will hug you more tightly. He
will not let you go, and you'll press your forehead against his neck, inhaling
his sweet musky scent of sweat and beer. He will say I love you, too. He will
call you honey and scold you for ever thinking that he didn't. You will not
know what to do, or if he'll remember this tomorrow.

There's no way I could've written this piece in first person; I tried and it scared
me too much. Instead, in my revisions I broke whatever rules I had to in order
to get the truth onto the page. In one draft I juggled first and second person,
and classmates couldn't make sense of what I was doing, so in the next I used
only second person. Though it seemed strange to be referring to myself as
"you," it was also very freeing. When it came time for final revisions, I tight-
ened sentences and cut out passive verbs, but I couldn't change the point of
view, because I thought I'd be hiding from readers part of my process of making sense of this experience.

The rules I think I break most frequently, however, are those applying to
content, the ones that suggest a good little writer wouldn't explore this topic or
make a character say or do such things. Erin Belieu sums up my feelings best
in her poem "High Lonesome": "My geography / is defined by those places / I
was told never to go" (2000, 17). The landscape of fiction—of all creative writing, really—should not be wholly familiar or safe. I don't feel as if I've done
my job as a writer if I haven't discovered something unexpected, haven't ended
up somewhere I've never been before or never even knew existed.

These rules I rebel against come to me in the voices of my high school
English teachers: Mrs. Morgan, a blonde version of Janet Reno with the waist-
band of her old-lady skirts hiked up to her abdomen, who loathed me because
I couldn't diagram sentences and did horribly on the standardized test for *The
Red Pony*; Mrs. Broderic, who forbade me from using the dash because she said
I used it far too much—ha! so there!—and who yelled at my eighth-grade
class for laughing at Romeo's bare behind in a bedroom scene of *Romeo and
Juliet*; Mrs. Horrell, who insisted so much more depended on William Carlos
Williams' red wheelbarrow than that it made the white chicken and the rain
beautiful, whose funny Johnstown accent made "film" come out like "feelm"
and "child" come out like "chald"; and Miss Devitz, skinny as an inchworm,
who made me change *ass* to *rear end* in a story before she'd submit it to a
regional contest, because the bishop couldn't possibly read my story with "an
expletive" in it.

Does it make me a bad person that I write to shock these four women? For
the love of God, I think they all need it! Allow me to clarify: I don't write to
offend anyone; I write to drop jaws only a little, to lower eyebrows or to raise
them, to make ultraconservative high school English teachers reread a page to

make sure they haven't misread something. Basically what I try to do is render characters honestly, and that sometimes entails showing a lover who's less than lovable or a father who acts far from paternal. When I work on early drafts, I sometimes hear the voice of a censor inside my head, telling me it's not polite to talk about such characters, and as a result I'll pull back from the shocking details. As I revise, however, I push myself to move beyond what my high school English teachers might expect; I try to use the sharpest, most original details for each character, even if they might not be the nicest or most politically correct ones.

This is certainly the case in my current fiction project: The narrator Mia's father left her family when she was in junior high school and hasn't acted particularly paternal to her ever since, though she's desperately wanted him to. In one scene from an unfortunately cast-off earlier draft, her father arrives for a visit several hours before he's supposed to. He finds Mia still groggy though it's late morning, and one of her (attractive male) coworkers sleeps on the couch in nothing but his boxer shorts.

My father stood on the front stoop, leaning close to the door, his fist balled to knock again, his tie-dye T-shirt spotted with rain, a tattered olive drab duffle bag slung over one shoulder. "Jesus, are you *deaf*? I've been out here for five minutes." He glanced over my shoulder. "Oh, you have company."

"You're early."

"And you're up to no good." He grinned. "Glad to see it. Do I need to go drive around for a while?"

"No." I stepped back. "Come in."

He let the screen door slam, and Spencer sat straight up, pressing his hands against the sides of his head while he gauged his surroundings. He saw me and blinked a little in acknowledgement.

"Morning." I didn't have to turn around to know my father was staring. "Coffee?"

Spencer nodded and mumbled something that sounded like *flowers*. Before I could ask, he gathered his clothes off the floor and shuffled down the hallway. The bathroom door squeaked shut, and, a few moments later, water whooshed from the showerhead.

"He drank too much last night. I wouldn't let him drive home."

"Right." My father nodded as he inspected the living room for evidence of furniture-warping sex. He seemed disappointed he didn't find any. "Hmm."

"We're not even seeing each other. We're just friends. We work together. He's my cameraman."

I stood in the center of the living room with my hands on my hips. Something was definitely wrong with this picture: here I was trying to justify why I *hadn't* had sex with the strange man my father discovered in my living room. Of course, Spencer wasn't that strange. I shook my head. My father still stared at me and smiled.

I hated having to sacrifice this scene, because I think it characterizes the father, Owen, perfectly. He's nothing but the atypical father, and writing scenes such as this one has given me the understanding of his character I need to drag him into subsequent drafts without sacrificing any of his mischievous charm.

Another way I've gone against the rules of, shall we say, good taste is to place otherwise good characters in what could be morally questionable situations. "Rental Kingdom," a story I wrote last spring, focuses largely on what happens within a character who finally works up the nerve to rebel against her parents. She passes up a medical internship to live in Galveston for the summer with a man she's not sure she loves or even wants to love. To show Tracy's awakening throughout the story, I tried making her increasingly aware of details that she wouldn't have noticed before living with Gus. As the story gains momentum, she speaks more honestly. This paragraph comes near the end:

> I wake later that night in an empty bed. . . . After I wipe the sleep from my eyes, the first thing I focus on is Gus standing on the balcony naked. This is nothing new; he often goes outside on hot nights like this in search of what little air might be circulating, and no one ever complains. We live behind a nudie bar, after all. Bare chests and asses in our neighborhood are nothing new. Full-frontal is a treat. What strikes me now, though, is the angle at which he stands, weight shifted to his right hip, shoulders slanted, head tilted.

Somehow I don't think this passage is ever going to end up on one of Mrs. Morgan's multiple-choice summer reading exams. What's important to me is that over the past year I've gained the confidence to write boldly. I write a first draft, then two or three days later I go back to it and read it aloud, marking places where it feels like I've flinched, that I've avoided having a character say something difficult or do something impulsive but true. Those are the places I return to in the next draft, and I continue this process (sometimes with four or five drafts) until every line rings as true as it can.

I no longer censor myself. I had to spend too many years holding myself back because I had teachers who wouldn't let me experiment with dashes or let my characters speak as they would in real life. High school showed me the damage that overly strict rules can do, the ways they can shut a young writer down and make him fear taking any risks whatsoever, and working with college freshmen hasn't changed that opinion.

Many students come to me believing that writing has a formula, that every essay or story can be written following the same conventions. What I push them to learn is that writing an essay is like going on a long car trip; you can take the interstate the whole way, flat and regular and boring, and get where you're going quickly and effortlessly. Or you can take side roads, where you might get lost and argue with your lousy navigator in the passenger seat and spend two and a half hours listening to an old-time preacher on AM radio, but those moments end up strengthening the trip. I make even my best students write several drafts, because I think they can always dig a little deeper, take a slightly different route than they already have. Writing is largely about *choices*, and I want my students to understand not only the rules of grammar and MLA—rules that are largely unbreakable—but what options they have every time they approach a writing assignment.

My problems with rules in writing, I've found, are largely my problems with organized religion, too. Writing, for me, is ultimately a way of finding meaning and discovering truth. And when it comes down to it, you can't do either of those things when you're obsessed with following every single rule. Immediately I want to feel guilty for suggesting that; I'm a writing teacher, after all, one who lowers grades for poor grammar and tangled wording. But I'm also a fallen Catholic; I took the whole damned sensual world when the devil offered it to me. Yes, I revise for style, so that readers can make sense of what I'm saying, but I focus more in later drafts on content, on making sure I'm facing every confrontation and painful event that the human psyche might try to make disappear.

Perhaps the biggest problem I had with the Catholic Church was its (ironically enough) unspoken rule *thou shalt not talk about problems, for then these problems will go away*. I've found that Catholicism is largely a religion of denial—denial of pleasure and denial of problems—and this repression has buried in me things I'll spend my whole life unearthing, tangled in or tarnished by guilt. I've finally learned to start using revision as a way of clearing away the filters and barriers that keep me from the clarity I want my writing to have.

Last June I began an essay about my former best friend that I planned to use for a nonfiction workshop. I still haven't been able to go back to the half-finished draft. I wanted to write it to try to make sense of what had happened to my relationship with my friend, when our joint quest to become better writers turned into a bitter rivalry, why our late nights of drinking turned into her alcoholism, how she misconstrued a close friendship for love and then cursed our mutual friend for spurning her advances.

In one passage, I finally manage to start speaking what's gone unspoken within me for far too long. At first I thought that by using poet Mark Doty's story, I was coming at my point indirectly, but he feels organic to me now:

> [Her] favorite poet is Lynda Hull, mine Mark Doty. It's strange and ironic—
> in the way that things always are with us, it seems—that Hull and Doty were
> themselves best friends for years. What I love about Doty is his grace, his ele-
> gance, but most of all his unflinching gaze. What [she] loves about Hull . . .
> is how she embraced ruined beauty. Doty, in his memoir *Heaven's Coast*,
> describes her as "a lover of appearances, of performances, of bravura, of
> failed but honorable gestures toward beauty. Because the world was ruined,
> wasn't it, and how could its children not be ruined as well?" (1996, 96)
>
> Hull's addictions to painkillers and alcohol strained her friendship with
> Doty. The day after his partner died of AIDS, she showed up at his house

drunk, and there, on the lip of the high-dive of grief, he had to confront her and tell her to leave. Months later, he met her outside her AA meeting to escort her to the restaurant where her husband was waiting, and he realized she was drunk again. During the small talk at lunch, he made a startling realization: "My friend, whom I've loved for years, my adventurer, wonderful poet, survivor, heroine, role model, flash girl, paragon of style and endurance—well, I find I just don't like her at all. How can I reclaim her?" (1996, 95)

He couldn't, not then, not ever. Not long after that awkward lunch, she smashed her white Saab into a tree along a Massachusetts highway. Later that evening, driving back from Boston on that same stretch of interstate, Doty encountered a detour. Something made him think *I wonder if it's someone I know,* though he wouldn't find out until the next morning that the tree Hull had hit smashed through the roof of her car and killed her instantly. Everything she left behind seemed in disarray: her friendship with Doty, her strained marriage to the poet David Wojahn, a just-finished manuscript in a black binder—what would become her posthumous collection *The Only World.* [My friend's] favorite book.

And while [she] isn't dead, she's dead to me, swallowed up by a city that reminds me of one of the outer circles of Dante's hell. Swallowed up by all the bottles of Johnny Walker she downed in three nights or less, all the glasses she smashed, all the letters she burned. What's so startling to me, though, is that I must've read that passage from Doty's memoir a dozen or more times, and not once did it ever make me think of [her] and me. Instead, I wondered how such close friends could let their relationship unravel.

. . . Lately I feel as if I've been studying with Lynda Hull. Ruined beauty. That's all that's left for the two of us; five years of practical jokes and late-night, front porch chats and pure joy at being alive dissolved by scotch whiskey and a man who may or may not have ever loved her and those same black words on white pages that once brought us together. To be honest, sometimes I'm still not sure how it happened.

I couldn't bring myself to finish this essay. Months later, some of the material from this essay surfaced in a poem about a romance that fell apart before I could even try to stop it. Once I drew the parallel between those relationships, I knew I'd gotten from this half-finished piece what I was meant to. I won't revise it to death; I know even unfinished, this draft has done what it was meant to.

The role style plays in this piece represents its role in my larger body of work. I am writing a story I don't want to tell, words that are supposed to go unspoken, old wounds that are supposed to be forgotten so that they can heal. At the same time, though, I draw courage to stay in these difficult moments from the way I render all their details, every sensual feature that brings these scenes off the page. Sometimes I find these details immediately; other times I struggle through draft after draft, remembering only the quality of light or the smell of lilacs before having to revise again.

But ultimately, Lynda Hull was right to celebrate ruined beauty. It's the simultaneous imperfection and splendor of everything—Gus naked on the balcony in the middle of the night, the rain gleaming on the blacktop when I walked out of the bar and never spoke to my best friend again. It's the only thing in this world that keeps us living, that keeps us writing, that keeps the rules from tearing us apart.

Works Cited

Belieu, Erin. 2000. *One Above and One Below*. Port Townsend, WA: Copper Canyon.

Doty, Mark. 1996. *Heaven's Coast*. New York: HarperCollins.

Seven

A Study in Sentence Style

Wendy Bishop

It's easy to imagine that we learn to write by joining words into sentences, sentences into paragraphs, and paragraphs into essays, reports, stories. In fact, that's how writing in school has most often been taught, as a lockstep accumulation of skills. Baby steps to giant steps. Part to whole. Basic to experimental. But any writer, like any carpenter (or mechanic, or cook, or artist, etc.), knows you need to put many of your skills in action simultaneously, just as you need many tools at once to frame a wall or raise a roof, to fix a car, to compose a stew, to assemble a collage, or to draft an essay.

We can't learn sentence patterns and just be done with them, because sentences are as infinite as the thoughts and ideas we would share through their use. Certainly some sentence basics can be named, no matter the language, but sound and sense, syntax (word order), and idea development take on new manifestations as each sentence is formed: *I ran into the house. I ran into the house, rapidly. I rapidly ran into the house. Rapidly, I ran into the house. I limped into the house. The dog and I walked into the house. Sinatra and I broke into the house. I walked and talked my way into the house. I ran into the house and then walked out into the garden through the unlocked and open French doors.* (OK, I'll stop now.)

The native speaker—and writer—of English learns to compose through practice and at a young age. But not by stringing word to word, sentence to sentence, and paragraph to paragraph. Linguistic knowledge is not merely additive (although it does add up eventually to literacy), it is generative. Communicative need pushed you onward. On that journey, you absorbed (language) community practices. For example, at a fairly predictable age, you discovered irregular verbs when you said, "I eated all my food," and were corrected to say, "I ate all my food," repeatedly. Some learn "I'm not going" and some learn "I ain't going" and later discover the first is standard practice and the second is dialect practice and that each signals something about speaking context and a speaker's language community, and more.

As a child language learner, if the rules you followed didn't yield results, you played with them, usually in the presence of doting experts who played back with you. Finding a situation when your abilities failed, you imitated what you thought you were hearing; in this way, your early sentences were patterned on the sentences of others but modified to your immediate needs. Regularly, in order to learn, you attempted what you couldn't yet accomplish and learned from supportive correction. Your sentences were generally well formed—"I want lion" (imagine small you in front of the zoo's lion exhibit)—even when you really didn't know what you were asking for. Later you learned it was communicative to say you admired the lion. You found your way into fluent language use by *using* language.

Generally, we understand conventions before we can name them. There are times, though, when articulating a choice is useful in allowing you to recognize similar choices in the future. The writer who wants to improve does so by experiment as well as by memorization. Anyone can embark on this course of study; it just requires careful reading and perhaps a file or journal page for copying down examples. To study sentences, pay attention to sentence relationships and practice sentence alteration and revision. Consider punctuation (as you will be encouraged to do in Chapter 8) and vocabulary choice as well as word order, repetition, and sentence-to-sentence cohesion and coherence. Note what happens when a proper name, *Humpty Dumpty,* is replaced by a common noun, *the egg,* for too long: you forget the speaker's or narrator's or character's name. Observe how a writer expands a metaphor across an entire paragraph (talking about writing as cooking and getting roast and onions and carrots and potatoes together as invention and revising as simmering the stew while adding the last ingredients, and finishing as serving up a plateful): Is the result elegant or heavy-handed? Lastly, have you ever noticed that careful transitions, strong causal relationships, and forceful parallel sentence patterns can support the logic of an unfolding argument?

If I could give you rules to follow to achieve these effects, I would. An inoculation of sentence sophistication. But there's no simple technique or advice that one writer can give to another to speed along sentence study. These moves have to be learned *in context,* by studying the sentences of writers you like and *by studying your own sentences.* Writers who want to see the rules at work in texts, or to name the rules and their exceptions, have to do so like the nonnative speaker, by memorizing a few of the sentence patterns that rhetoricians—those who study spoken and written communication—and linguists have named, practicing them in writing, and actively looking to find them at work in the writing they read.

To learn the possibilities of sentences, you need to be attentive and inventive. You have to trust in your basic tool kit—your well-developed ear for the language—even if you don't have a highly technical vocabulary to describe what you see on the page.[1] Sentences both please and challenge writers. "Well, very often, once I get to the revising, at least two or three words per line just give me grief," claims June Jordan, "they won't budge because they say, 'No,

---

1. Those who are not native speakers have a reverse set of skills (and needs)—an ability to name learned sentence patterns but a greater need to practice them in context to internalize idiomatic and irregular and dialectical expression.

I'm staying here,' and I say, 'Yeah, but you're not right!'" I expect, like me, like Jordan, you've talked back to your writing, begging a sentence or paragraph or stanza to just give you a break and work right.

Instead, study sentences by considering some of the exercises—some with examples—that follow. You'll imitate other published writers, imitate other peer writers, and imitate sentence patterns and incorporate some of those patterns into your current or future drafts. The first two techniques do not require that you learn rules or name them, although having a language to talk about writing choices is always useful and, if you turn professional, perhaps essential. The third technique offers you a selection of prenamed common patterns that you can try.

Imitating Published Writers

Two writing teacher writers prepared this argument in favor of imitation. I return after their discussion with related exercises. Like them, you might begin by remembering your own experiences with imitating writing.

Carlyn Maddox and Carissa Neff
On Imitation

I.

During my freshman year at the University of Idaho, I took a poetry class from Marta Mihalyi—an exuberant and slight woman whose eyes flickered when she talked and gesticulated about passion and the art of seeing and strong verbs. I was an English major, but in no other class was I given the task to imitate, which surprises me now, for it was tremendously helpful. And fun. Marta, for our first assignment, gave us the poem "We Real Cool," by Gwendolyn Brooks. I had never read the poem before. Had I?

She read the poem aloud, tapped her foot to the rhythms. She then asked us to come up with our own versions of Brooks' poem, but insisted we keep the meter. I went home and wrote "We Real Cold" (I was in Idaho, after all). When we met for the next class, everyone read his or her version aloud, taking turns, nervous and excited, laughing and clapping. The air was electric. Something had happened. Our own eyes flickered. Through imitation, we learned to create poems of our own. Though this activity helped us connect to Brooks' voice and initiate our own work, simply imitating her rhythm, syntax, and structure was just as exciting as seeing the end result of our own poems. "We Real Cold" was a morph of my voice and Brooks' style, and the energy of those feelings that "I too can create something like this" was a powerful and instructive tool in my apprenticeship as a writer. This built confidence and offered me a window into my own vision on the page.

2.

For several years, I have been intrigued and inspired by the works of Michael Ondaatje. Best known for the Booker Prize–winning *English Patient*, his prose weaves poetics, narrative, and lyricism together in a story of four war-ravaged people living together during the final days of World War II. I was so taken with his compelling prose that I often copied whole chapters in an effort to somehow plug into his voice and hoped it would miraculously "rub off" on me.

Here is a passage I often copied and imitated:

> They are in the botanical garden, near the Cathedral of All Saints. She sees one tear and leans forward and licks it, taking it into her mouth. As she has taken the blood from his hand when he cut himself cooking for her. Blood. Tear. He feels everything is missing from his body, feels he contains smoke. All that is alive is the knowledge of future desire and want.

And here is one imitation of mine from [a story titled] "Firsts":

> They stand in the bathroom of the Oakland Coliseum, escaping the raucous A's game outside the thin, white walls. He takes her shoulders in his hands, crushing them against a stall door, wanting possession of her bones, the destiny of her love. He breathes in her scent, breathes in the fear and excitement pulsing from her skin. All that is alive between them is awkward and electric.

Here I imitate Ondaajte's rhythms and structure, but the content, the story, comes from my own vision. Imitating another's work can provide the impetus to create a similar work, but ultimately we must put our particular spin on that style and form something new. Many times, as seen with Ondaajte's work, the style isn't as imitated as much as the tone or atmosphere of the piece; we engage with a person's dream and want to re-create this dream for ourselves. Imitation, then, is a form of conversation, a "talking back" or a "dialogic dreamspace" we enter in order to learn and create from our sense of meaning and language.

3.

Through imitation, writers—old and new—are then better able to practice not only the tone and atmosphere of any given piece but the syntactical structures and elements of voice—the overall style, we might say. Yet, because style is the umbrella under which elements like voice and tone play, the individual writer, or imitator here, would face a near impossibility if she were to try to mimic exactly a Brooks poem or Ondaatje's prose paragraph. A writer might be able to imitate a voice or a syntax or a rhythm or a tone, but what is the nameless ingredient that is impossible to imitate? For, as literary history has shown, writers who try to take on a Faulknerian voice, or who are heavily influenced by, say, Hemingway, often cannot imitate the host writer exactly. We might ask ourselves why this is so in order to learn how the action of imitation actually works to oftentimes enhance a writer's individual style. When an imitator "talks back" to the writer she is imitating, what is gained precisely?

The act of imitating often leads to creation of new work, and this is a valuable practice to follow when first learning how sentences, paragraphs, and entire works act as units of imagery or thought. Through "talking back" to texts, the writer can master techniques and strategies from the original piece, but the writer must provide that other unique ingredient that elucidates his or her personal vision and experience. Paul Cezanne, the famous French Impressionist, said, "Style is not created through servile imitation of the masters; it proceeds from the artist's own particular way of feeling and expressing himself." It is this expression that spins a new twist on anything imitated, and a writer can often be led to an original voice through this imitation of an author's structure or tone. Imitation of another's work, then, cannot be a substitute for the writer's imagination or personal "style," but it certainly offers the writer stylistic and structural ideas to attempt.[2]

Memorization and imitation used to be standard forms of language instruction, forms that were abused when schoolchildren were set to recitations in order to inculcate good manners and also keep them occupied and out of the teacher's hair. When used for control or intimidation—"Here, copy this Picasso and then tell me if you really believe you can paint!"—these practices can have a devastating effect on learners. However, most writers admit that they do learn a great deal from imitation. From hearing people speak and capturing those cadences in their prose. From being read to as children and finding lifelong pleasure in capturing their own visions of the world in prose. By comparing—like painter with model with canvas—their memory of a powerful or innovative piece of writing with their own writing on the screen. Writers derive, borrow, adapt, transform, translate, steal (in the positive sense), transmute, turn inside out, contend with, seek to top, rework the writings of others: plot, argument, sentence structure, vocabulary, sound, organization . . . anything that can be done in writing can be—and is—imitated. To benefit from imitation for revision, use it as a jump start, not a straightjacket. You'll find it most useful to focus on imitating and revising for style at the sentence level using a current text. Later you can decide to apply what you learn, or not, to future texts. So now some sentence journeys.

Exercises in Imitation

1.   Characterize the prose style of your favorite authors by figuring out their sentencing practices. Writers rely on long sentences, short sentences, compound and complex, or try to mix their sentencing in rhythmic and unpredictable ways. Some writers sound stuffy and some overly sweet. What makes a piece of writing welcoming and friendly or off-putting and grim? Collect a typical-of-that-author paragraph for several writers you admire and imitate them in one, or both, of these ways.

2. Thanks to the writers quoted here as well as all other members of the Spring 2003 Style Seminar for your dedicated sentence study and generous permission to share what you taught me.

a. Compose an original paragraph of your own that echoes or mimics the target paragraph closely by imitating sentencing choices (punctuation, parallel words or clauses, repetition, rhyme, length, and so on).

b. Take a paragraph of your own and see if you can revise it to echo the target paragraph's sentences as much as possible while trying to improve your prose.

The following writers were imitating samples of *conspicuous style* (writing that called attention to the writing technique used) and *clear style*. In the first example, the writer offers a target paragraph and follows with his own paragraph in the manner of exercise 1a:

Target Paragraph: Conspicuous Style

The whole passionate enigma of life, the living contradiction, the indemonstrable but over whelming unity which comprises every antithesis by which men live and die, is evoked by the spirit of Spring as by no other season. And yet, to the young man, this time of year often seems to be the time of chaos and confusion. For him it is the time of the incoherence of the senses, the wild, tongueless cries of pain, joy, and hunger, the fierce, broken wanderings of his desire, the lust for a thousand unknown and unnamable things which maddens his brain, disturbs his vision, and rends his heart asunder.
—Thomas Wolf, *The Web and the Rock*

Imitation Paragraph

That crazy thing we call love, the joy felt after crying because of distance, the unconditional quality of its being, the last true experience we feel before dying, is defined only by the parameters of our consenting desire to love and be loved. And yet, to the heartbroken, this sensation becomes nothing more than an experience of heartburn and pain. For her it's King Arthur's sword slicing the core of her being, leaving her voiceless, desireless, vindictive, outraged.
—Kenya

The next writer provides a passage that seemed clear to her and then revised her own paragraph in imitation, as in exercise 1b. After completing this exercise, the writer may see the imitative pattern far more clearly than the reader, since the writer is trying to use *some* of the target author's sentence structures but also improve her original text.

Target Paragraph: Clear Style

These were good days for me. I was nineteen years old and this was the hardest work I had ever done. The days were stunning, starting hot and growing insistently hotter. My first week two of the days had been 116. The heat was a pure physical thing, magnified by the steel and pavement of the plant, and in that first week, I learned what not to touch, where not to stand, and I found the powerhouse heat simply bracing. I lost some of the winter dormitory

fat and could feel myself browning and getting into shape. It felt good to pull on my Levis and work shoes every morning (I'd tossed my tennies after the nail incident), and not to have any papers due for any class.
—Ron Carlson, "Oxygen"

Imitation

I am worried about my brother, Stephen. He is forty years old, separated from his wife, and probably sees too many beer cans around his Lazy Boy every morning. He has written only one letter to the family, and in it he stated in his usual stiff-lipped way the following: "I go to the house every two weeks, mow the grass, pay the bills. We don't talk much. There isn't much to say." He hasn't returned my calls, so I'm writing letters instead. He wrote back once and said "I'm not a gloomy gus, but I do have the demon rum." "Things," he added,"will work out fine." But I want to ask him what things, Stephen? What "things" will work out? I want to tell him of my own demons, but this is his story in our letters, not mine. . . .
—Carlyn

The move from imitation to parody happens naturally and actually repre-sents expert stylistic reading on the part of the imitator. The following passage parodies the opening of Virginia Woolf's novel *Mrs. Dalloway*. It was com-posed by Maggie Gerrity (whom you met in Chapter 6), using Jay Szczepanski (whom you'll meet in chapter 12), her office mate, and mutual friends Kate and Peter as characters:

Mr. Szczepanski should have planned the party himself.

For Kate had her work cut out for her. The guests had to be informed; the Computer Writing Center teachers were coming. And then, thought Jay Szczepanski, what a morning—humid as if issued to a weather forecaster or hurricane chaser.

What a stink! What a bust! For it had always seemed to him, when, with a little squeak of the desk chair, which he could hear now, he had burst out of the cubicle and plunged at the office into the dank air. How stale, how tense, closer than this of course, the office was early in the morning; like the thud of a boot, the stomp of a foot; resonant and absolute yet (for a boy of 23 as he then was) permanent, feeling as he did standing there at the office window, that another awful birthday was about to happen; look-ing at the staplers, at the computers with heat rising off their monitors and their keyboards clacking, clicking; standing and looking until Peter Reed said, "Musing among the office supplies?"—was that it?—"I prefer men to tape dispensers"—was that it? He must have said it in pedagogy work-shop when he had gone out into the computer writing classroom—Peter Reed. He would be back from 1101 one of these days, Thursday or Friday, he forgot which, for his emails were awfully dull; it was his sayings one groaned at; his glasses, his flip flops, his toothy grin, his goofiness and,

when millions of things had utterly vanished—how funny it was!—a few
sayings about staplers.

Maggie momentarily joins a line of Woolf imitators, most recent of whom is
Michael Cunningham in the novel *The Hours,* which was transformed into an
Academy Award–wining movie of the same name. And she, like others, learns
about Woolf's sentence sense through parody.

2. Another way to gain insight into sentence-level style is to create a self-referencing definition of style types: chatty, confiding, clear, obscure, hyperbolic,
and other sorts of styles. *Self-referencing* means the text both defines and illustrates the type of writing under discussion. For instance, Ernest Hemingway's
style is so strikingly unadorned that it could be called "plain style" by those who
admire clarity and simplicity or "primer prose" by those who find stark and
unadorned literary writing simplistic and unsophisticated. In her definition,
Rawan illustrates, defines, and also adds texture by imitating the language of
"Run Jane Run" readers and (stereotyped) kindergarten teachers:

Primer Prose

This is a paragraph. See the paragraph? It is a simple paragraph. The words
are simple. See the words? The sentences are simple. See the sentences?
Many simple words. Many simple sentences. This is a very simple paragraph. It has exclamation points! Does it have questions? Yes it does. See the
questions? Questions are marked with a curly line and a dot. That is how we
know it is a question. Exclamations are marked with a straight line and a dot.
An exclamation is a loud sentence. The sentences are still simple. They are
simply louder than regular sentences. The way we know to read them loudly
is by looking at the straight line and the dot! See the line and the dot? Yes,
you see them! Is there suspense? There is not really suspense. It is very predictable. That is nice! No surprises.

—Rawan

a. Compose a serious self-referencing paragraph for primer prose. It will
   help if you call it "Plain Style" to avoid the primary connotations.

b. Compose a parody and a serious self-referencing definition for conspicu-
   ous style (think Thomas Wolf, William Faulkner, Gertrude Stein,
   Jamaica Kincaid, and others whose *sentencing* is particularly noticeable).
   First define conspicuous style by writing a parodic conspicuous para-
   graph. Then compose a more serious version, which you title "Ornate
   Style" or "Complex Prose" or another accurate title of your choosing.

Imitating Peer Writers

We get intimidated by famous writers if we feel we can never match up to their
work. We get bored by famous writers if we find their subject or (sentence) style

unexciting. That's why imitating the work of peers or near contemporaries can teach some writers more . . . at first. Peers have similar interests and language. Their texts should join your collection of interesting texts.

Exercises for Imitating Peers

3.   To begin, it never hurts to analyze your own style, in your own words. You don't need the correct handbook term for split infinitive to use or avoid one, but you should be able to describe the difference between "to help wash the car" and "help to wash the car" if you find that the first is a common pattern in your writing (you may have already learned that that pattern bothers some readers).

a.   Analyze your sentence patterns by reviewing one *representative* piece of writing. Consider the moves you make, especially those you rely on or repeat (the chart in Appendix A at the end of this chapter may help you with this project). Do you use one-word transitions and only one-word transitions? Do you always work to include great modifiers? Too many rhetorical questions? Heavy use of parallel sentence patterns? List all the sentence moves you can see and hear when you read your writing aloud. Use sentence examples to illustrate your list.

b.   Study your style by reviewing multiple pieces of your own writing. If you've been writing for a while, you know that certain sorts of writing issues challenge you. Look for illustrations of where you've managed to rise to the challenge (or not):

> As a stylist, I am particularly interested in language use, especially conveying accent or dialect (place) not so much through creative spellings (e.g., "warsh" for "wash," or "yay-up" for "yep"), but through turns of phrase or colloquialisms. Some examples from one of my stories:
>
> "She sighed—one of those sounds that means she sees something so beautiful she can't hardly breathe for looking at it."
>
> "It's Dis Gusting. Right in front of everyone, holding hands with her . . . lover."
>
> "She had done it so quick and graceful, you kind of had to admire her."
>
> "She took it from me real slow, like it was a religion or something."
>
> —Debi

c.   Follow your sentence-style self-analysis with a discussion of *why* and *how* you feel you developed your practices and on what you base your beliefs:

> As I mentioned earlier, I prefer simplicity, even when it comes to sentences. Why would I want to use complex forms when a simple sentence form could do the job? Read *Ulysses* by Joyce and you might find yourself in a paradise of compound sentences, but the more you read and the

more they go on, you will find yourself screaming: "For heaven's sake
James, use a period." Or what about the stream of consciousness gang!
Yes, I bet they would make good pickpockets, you do not even feel or
notice that they have moved from one character's head to another's.
They do that with their long windy compound structured sentences.
   —Fadi

4.   Try collaborative peer imitation. You and a partner each compose your own
initial paragraph—nonfiction or fiction—on any subject you want. Write this full
paragraph in your normal style. Send it to the other writer by email. Each of you
extends the other's discussion or story (even poem—swap stanzas) and sends it
back to the originating author. Complete two rounds (four paragraphs) minimum;
continue on if you have time. The last author should try to provide a satisfying
conclusion. Exchange your two drafts (one started by you, one started by your
partner) with a second pair of writers who are doing the same collaborative
style experiment. As you will do with their drafts, they will try to decide

a.   who began each sequence, based on which textual clues, and

b.   if they can describe any difference between one coauthored text (begun
     by you) and the other (begun by your partner).

Here's a sample to practice with, composed by Fadi Al-Issa and me. I don't provide the author identification that is available on a second sample, a coauthored
short story by Carlyn Maddox and Carissa Neff, which you'll find in Appendix
B at the end of this chapter.

If Only It Were Like Eating a French Fry

I don't know about the rest of you, but when I intentionally begin reading a
paper for revision, I find it harder to point out things that actually need to be
revised. I usually read, reread and do more reading. However, when I stop
thinking about this process and begin doing something else like watching TV
that is when it hits me, and then I go back to a certain point and do a good job
on revising it. It takes a longer time but it is more constructive. It is just like
eating French fries. You pick the fry up, dip it in ketchup and then stare at it
from different angles before taking the decision of eating it. Sometimes we end
up throwing it away because we did not like the way it looked, or we just
remove the extra salt off it, or we pick up another one because this one is too
small and we do not want to waste that energy of chewing on a small French
fry. Do we think about this, do we say OK first I have to examine it, and then
decide on what to do? Nevertheless, we always end up with a good decision.
So if we can find a way to make revision a less conscious process, I think the
results would be better and there would be less stress while doing it. And do
not tell me you never stared at a French fry before eating it. [author?]

   For that matter, don't tell me you don't revise. I think we all revise.
Although, perhaps, some of us just do it without thinking about what revision

means to us. And when we do think about it, we tend to fuss about scale. For
some of us, revision is like making French fries, from scratch. We have a
potato but we don't know at first it's going to be French fries so we think about
all the potato dishes we like: mashed, French fried, boiled with a little butter.
This depends on the sort of potato we managed to buy. We may have a Yukon
gold, Idaho, new red in our hand. Sometimes, in fact it's the potato that deter-
mines the revision. Sometimes a potato becomes a poem or story or essay.
Some of us always know that we're going to end up in the frozen food section of the market. You stare at Ida-Ore bags or any other bright plastic bag
and you decide, OK, thin sliced or thick sliced or crinkle cut? You already
knew you wanted to eat French fries all along. You're not a mashed potatoes
kind of guy. I don't know if you're less stressed now, but you're thinking about
pleasure not about outcomes. Still, do not tell me you can not tell the difference between a home made and a fresh frozen French-fry. (author?)

And if you do not know the difference between the homemade and the
fresh frozen one, then you will need to work on your taste. That is easy.
Take a bowl, make sure it is clean, and then add both kinds into it. Mix them
together. Try to clear your mind of all preexisting notions concerning French
fries. After that just try to concentrate on what you perceive as you taste. Try
to repeat it again and see if you can find a better way to distinguish the two
tastes. Attempt to add some seasoning in order to make it a little bit tougher.
What? You want to take another go? I guess you are in the process of revising your techniques to find which one suits you the most and helps clarify and
distinguish originality from imitation. That is the yellow brick road to revision. It all starts with those yellow golden fries. [author?]

And sidle down the road, with me, or is that slide off the arch and let's
get back to business? Doesn't revision improve your palate? Do you think
about food consciously? You bet you do. So why not writing? Or French fries?
We're aware and not aware of what we do when we eat a French fry. We know
we like them hot and fresh and with ketchup (some of us) and salt (some of
us), and we don't like to think much about making them ourselves (some of
us), but then all that isn't true either. At least once in your life, shouldn't you
try making perfect French fries from scratch? Just to know what it means. And
taste testing and sampling is fun too. By mixing our samples together, evaluating them, considering them, throwing some away, hell, just by looking at
French fries, we learn more. We become gourmands. Or at least hungry writers, welcome at many tables. [author?]

Imitating Traditional Sentence Patterns

The stuff of sentences is not new to us, but we may not have a comfortable language for talking about what it is we read on the page or hear in our heads. I
expect you use *anaphora* and *metaplasmus* all the time without realizing it. You
do other things like balancing your sentence clauses or choosing your words

for sound as well as meaning. You know that the choice between *rain* and *downpour* matters; it represents the difference between a broad category of weather and an intense manifestation of weather from that category. Writers aim for precision, but they're also influenced by the music words make together. Should you choose *sudden shower; wreaking rainy havoc; loose and stingy showers; a restless rain?* You'll have to—get to—decide.

It's easy to forget that we also subvocalize as we read, and listen to sentences in our heads. Eudora Welty describes how important the practice of reading her own sentences became: "Ever since I was first read to, then started reading to myself, there has never been a line read that I didn't *hear.* As my eyes followed the sentence, a voice was saying it silently to me. It isn't my mother's voice, or the voice of any person I can identify, certainly not my own. It is human, but inward, and it is inwardly that I listen to it. It is to me the voice of the story or the poem itself. . . ." In interviews, writers often claim that they couldn't begin a text until they found the first line or the last line or heard their character talking. When I read this observation by Welty, I realize I connect these claims to moments of internal composition and revision.

At the end of this chapter, you'll find references to several books that can help you expand on the whirlwind tour of sentence pattern exercises we're about to undertake at this point.

Sentence Pattern Exercises

5.   Consider the many ways you can use repetition in your prose by eavesdropping on this student of style's notes on repetition. Carissa includes definitions, professional examples, and her own examples. Making your own stylebook of this sort joins you to a long tradition of apprentice writers (going back to ancient Greek rhetoricians).

Repepepepetition

Major Kinds:

Anaphora—Repetition at beginning of a sentence.

Epistrophe—Repetition at the end of a sentence.

Symploce—Beginning and ending sentences with the same words.

Epanalepsis—Beginning and ending sentences with same word.

Inclusio—Beginning and ending a longer passage with the same (group of) word(s).

Anadiplosis—Ending one sentence and beginning the next with the same word.

Gradatio—A chain, or stair-step, of Anadiploses.

Illustration

Anaphora—from Thoreau's Walden *(emphasis added):*
NOT EVEN rats in the wall, for they were starved out, or rather were never

baited in,—only squirrels on the roof and under the floor, a whippoorwill on
the ridge pole, a blue-jay screaming beneath the window, a hare or woodchuck
under the house, a screech-owl or a cat-owl behind it, a flock of wild geese
or a laughing loon on the pond, and a fox to bark in the night [a great example here, too, of a- and poly-syndetons]. NOT EVEN a lark or an oriole,
those mild plantation birds, ever visiting my clearing. NO cockerels to crow
nor hens to cackle in the yard. NO yard! but unfenced Nature reaching up to
your very sills.

From Louise Erdrich's Love Medicine:
HER skin is glowing, as if she were brightly golden beneath the brown. HER
hair is dry and electric. . . . Turning to me, HER mouth a tight gleaming tri-
angle, HER cheekbones high and pointed, HER chin a little cup, HER eyes
lit, she watches.

Epanalepses from Kurt Vonnegut's Slaughterhouse 5:
Out of the showerheads gushed scalding RAIN. THE RAIN was a blowtorch that did not warm.

Gradatio—stair-step repetition—from John Steinbeck's The Pearl:
But Kino's brain burned, even during his sleep, and HE DREAMED that
Coyotito could read, that one of his own people could tell him the truth of
things. And in HIS DREAM, Coyotito was reading from a book as large as
a house, with letters as big as dogs, and the words galloped and played on the
book. And then DARKNESS spread over the page, and with the DARK-
NESS came the music of evil again, and Kino STIRRED in his sleep; and
when he STIRRED, Juana's eyes opened in the DARKNESS. And then Kino
awakened, with the evil music pulsing in him, and he lay in the DARK-
NESS with his ears alert.

My own examples

Anaphora

She wanted more than his presence; she wanted his conversation and laugh-
ter; she wanted his fears and insecurities and troubles; she wanted to get
inside of him like a tick that refused to be burned out.

Epistrophe

Most of their close moments, most of their lives, happened in that bed. They,
of course, slept in that bed together for 25 years, but they also made children
in that bed, fought in that bed, laughed and cried and read novels and newspapers in that bed. They ate breakfast in that bed, fed each other soup during illness in that bed, had vomited and recovered in that bed. To get rid of
that bed would mean getting rid of their lives, and Annie wouldn't have it.

Symploce

I cried for the island. The island where I'd grown up. I'd grown up and up.
Up to the orange and red skies. Red skies so bloody, the clouds must have
been murdered. Murdered until they fell dead black. Black disappearing and
dissolving to stars.

Undertake a similar exploration, through one of the following exercises.

a. Begin with your own sentence patterns; look up names for the sentence structure in some of the books I reference; at the end of this chapter look for published examples (you can roam more broadly than fiction writers for this); and share their samples. That's the reverse of Carissa's method.

b. Or, like Carissa, find some interesting terms in the books I list at the end of the chapter, find published examples, and find examples in your own writing. If you don't find the pattern in your own writing, now is the time to try it. Imitate the published example to create your own.

6. Choose sentence patterns that sound obscure or for which you simply like the name (*zeugma* is one of my favorites). Practice the same pattern—definition, published example, your example—outlined in exercises 5a or 5b.

> **Tmesis**—Breaking a word in two, usually to put another word between the parts.
> *Examples:*
> Abso-bloody-lutely
> Pick-em-up Truck
> Absofreakinlutely!
>
> **Hyperbaton**—Any intended deviation from ordinary word order.
> *Examples:*
> "When nine hundred years old you reach, look as good you will not, hm?"
> —Yoda, *Return of the Jedi*

7. Compile your own sentence pattern crib sheet—something to keep by the computer to sometimes refer to as a way of enlarging your revision options. Carissa's is based on a text by Arthur Quinn, hence her shorthand for these sentence patterns—"Quinns."

> For my own purposes, I have created an easy reference for the different Quinns. I do this for my bad memory. I often hope to recognize Quinns in context over the course of my daily reading, but it rarely happens. I forget the names first, and then I forget the Quinn altogether. I am often thumbing through the book wondering "where in the hell I saw that." And, as an aside, I am turned off by Arthur's relentless use of biblical examples. Therefore, I created this list so I don't have to reference the book all of the time, trying to make sense of bible verses in order to make sense of the Quinn being exemplified. Oh, I do go on. Forgive me.
>   Maybe the reference will be helpful for others.
> 1. **enallage:** An effective grammatical mistake. Ex: "We was robbed!" (5)
> 2. **asyndeton:** Omission of an expected conjunction. Ex: "I came, I saw, I conquered." (7)

3. **polysyndeton:** Many conjunctions. Ex: We ate rice and lamb and naan and cucumbers and yogurt. (11)

4. **paradiastole:** Polysyndeton of "or" or "nor." Ex: Swim or sink or die. (13)

5. **hendiadys:** Addition of a conjunction between an adjective and a noun, accompanied usually by the rearrangement of the order of the adjective and noun. Also uses "and" to split a thing into two or three or more. Ex: "By force and (by) arms." (16, 25)

6. **metaplasmus:** Purposefully misspelling. Ex: "Gawd" for "God." (19)

7. **brachylogia:** Like asyndeton, but omission of a conjunction between words or phrases. Ex: I went to the doctor and then I became ill, sick to my stomach. (21)

8. **prosthesis:** A type of prefix added to the beginning of a word. Ex: "enskied." (21)

9. **epenthesis:** Added to the middle of a word. Ex: "the visitating sun." (21)

10. **proparalepsis:** Added to the end of a word. Ex: "our climature." (22)

11. **aphaearesis:** Subtracting from the beginning of a word. Ex: "The king hath cause to plain." (22)

12. **syncope:** Subtracting from the middle of a word. Ex: "Home art gone, and ta'en thy wages." (22)

13. **apocope:** Subtracting from the end of a word. Ex: "When I ope my lips." (22)

14. **synaloepha:** Omission of a vowel in a contraction. Ex: "Take't; 'tis yours. What is't?" (22)

15. **antisthecons:** All letter substitutions. Ex: "Come, go we then togither." (23)

16. **metatheses:** Rearrangements of letters. Ex: "With liver burning hot. Frevent." (23)

17. **ellipses:** Omission of words, not necessarily denoted by ". . ." Ex: "The man, [who is] the lord of the land." (27)

18. **zeugma:** THIS IS WHERE I NOTICE THAT THERE IS ALREADY A QUICK REFERENCE SHEET ON PAGE 101. Sheesh.

Crib sheets work. Practice illuminates. Sentence journals make sense. Making your own list is instructive; as you type out definitions and examples, the sentence shape becomes more concrete. It becomes an option that is open to you. And while you're at it, look up and illustrate *zeugma*.

Who Benefits?

We tend to imagine only poets focus on words, word order, and sentence patterns and revise them to this degree. But writers are obsessed with the sentence: "What I know about grammar is its infinite power. To shift the structure of a sentence alters the meaning of that sentence," claims Joan Didion, "as definitely and inflexibly as the position of a camera alters the meaning of the object photographed. Many people know about camera angles now, but not so many know about the sentence." And there's power in gaining knowledge in this area.

Perhaps you feel more comfortable talking camera angles than sentence options, but I'll argue my case this way: You know about camera angles because you watch film and view still and moving images and tacitly pick up techniques. You imitate and you practice when you get caught up in photography, whether you're an amateur or an expert. You take lots of snaps, more than ever now that the art has gone digital. I suggest you do the same with your sentences (and the word processor speeds you on this journey). Imitate patterns you admire. Learn a comfortable vocabulary for naming some of those effects. Play with some of those effects in your own work.

Language learners often mention that after immersion and practice, they begin to dream in their second language; I believe sentence explorations turn around for you one day in a similar manner: you become more fluent, you *see* and *hear* your sentences on several levels and in this manner prepare yourself to dream up new and better ones.

Works Cited and for Further Reading

Burrows, Terry. 2001. *Txt Tlk: Hw2 Tlk w/o Bng Hrd.* Ferndale, WA: Carlton.

Christensen, Francis. 1963. "A Generative Rhetoric of the Paragraph." *College Composition and Communication* 16(3): 144–61.

Connors, Robert J. 2000. "The Erasure of the Sentence." *College Composition and Communication* 52: 96–128.

Corbett, Edward P. J. 1971. "The Theory and Practice of Imitatio in Classical Rhetoric." *College Composition and Communication* 22: 243–50.

Corbett, Edward P. J., and Robert J. Connors. 1999. *Classical Rhetoric for the Modern Student.* 4th ed. New York: Oxford University Press.

Danet, Brenda. 2001. *Cyberpl@y: Communicating Online.* Oxford, NY: Berg.

Harris, Robert A. 2003. *Writing with Clarity and Style: A Guide to Rhetorical Devices for Contemporary Writers.* Los Angeles: Pyrczak.

Johnson, T. R. 2003. *A Rhetoric of Pleasure: Prose Style and Today's Composition Classroom.* Portsmouth, NH: Boyton/Cook.

Laib, Nevin K. 1993. *Rhetoric and Style: Strategies for Advanced Writers.* New Jersey: Prentice Hall.

Loux, Ann. 1981. "Using Imitations in Literature Classes." *College Composition and Communication* 38: 466–72.

Mander, Gabrielle. 2001. *Wan2Tlk? Ltl Bk of Txt Msgs.* St. Martin's.

Minock, Mary. 1995. "Towards a Postmodern Pedagogy of Imitation." *Journal of Advanced Composition* 15(3): 489–509.

Quinn, Arthur. 1993. *Figures of Speech: Sixty Ways to Turn a Phrase.* Davis, CA: Hermagoras.

Weathers, Winston. 1980. *An Alternate Style: Options in Composition*. Rochelle Park, NJ: Hayden.

———. 1985. "The Winston Weathers Writing Way: A Self-Examination." *Writers on Writing*, ed. Tom Waldrop. New York: Random House.

Appendix A

Features of Prose Style

First, let us set down, in outline form, a list of the features that you can look for when analyzing prose style.

A. Kind of diction
    1. general or specific
    2. abstract or concrete
    3. formal or informal
    4. Latinate (usually polysyllabic) or Anglo-Saxon (usually monosyllabic)
    5. common words or jargon
    6. referential (denotative) or emotive (connotative)

B. Length of sentences (measured in number of words)

C. Kinds of sentences
    1. grammatical: simple, compound, complex, compound-complex
    2. rhetorical: loose, periodic, balanced, antithetical
    3. functional: statement, question, command, exclamation

D. Variety of sentence patterns
    1. inversions
    2. sentence openers
    3. method and location of expansion

E. Means of articulating sentences (coherence devices)

F. Use of figures of speech

G. Paragraphing
    1. length (measured in number of words and number of sentences)
    2. kind of movement or development in paragraphs
    3. use of transitional devices (Corbett and Connors 1999, 361)

Appendix B

Collaborating on Fiction

Carlyn and Carissa's collaborative fiction piece: "Keeping Score." (One writer begins and the next continues the story, trying to keep the style more or less consistent; writers alternate by paragraphs or roughly equal units.)

Keeping Score

This morning Mr. Hurst drops me off last at the Southeastern Nursing Home, parks the school van near the front entrance, and catches my wrist before I can jump out. Hold up, Becca, he says, but I warn him it's not pretty what I'm thinking and yank my hand back quick so he won't see how my arm's raked with red cuts. He sighs, pressing his palms into the wheel, and my stomach coils into a fist. If he starts up about Roddey, or my parents, or the total joke of his "fresh start" school for special kids like me, I swear he can kiss his volunteer reader to the old farts goodbye. No more Leviticus readings to emphysemic Ms. Shad in 5B or feeding *Reader's Digest* gruel to Mr. Pooler in 10D. . . . But I can feel a lecture coming on, the way I know a storm's coming even when there's no clouds and only a trace of wind. He turns to me, his small eyes narrowing like he's trying to size me into a girl that's understandable. I look away, like I always do—away and beyond the moment—and press my arm to my T-shirt, the welts still live and tender. [Carlyn]

Mr. Hurst looks away too, doesn't say anything right away, just turns and stares out the windshield at the clouds moving in. I see my chance to get away and almost succeed. Facing the Nursing Home, my back to the van and its open door, I hear him like he's in the back of my head or something. . . . I used to hate myself too. I don't look back when I hear the van door latch shut or the tires working the gravel drive. I don't look back as I hear the van's acceleration into traffic. I am good at resisting urges like that. I am good at covering things up. The rain rolls in fast, quickens my pace to the entrance of The Home. It's 3:15—I'm supposed to be here at 3:00 to get my hours. Mrs. Cunningham sits behind the front desk like a fat sack of potatoes and greets me with the raise of an eyebrow—plucked nearly to nonexistence—and a ball point pen chained to a clip board. I brace for her lecture by giving her an I-don't-give-a-shit yawn . . . but I do give a shit. No one believes me, but I do. [Carissa]

"Late," Mrs. C says, tapping the clip board and shooting me this suspicious glare. "Ms. Shad's been asking about you."

I don't say anything, and thankfully she doesn't launch into some spiel about my hours. She then hands me the form I'm supposed to sign. All these check-ups on me, and for what? I got caught with one joint, one friggin' joint in my book bag, and the whole world stops. Now I have to sign forms like these and go to Hurst's school and learn about anger management and student behavior. Now I gotta have some explanation for everything I feel and think—like I really have a clue into all of that anyway.

"Just plan to stay an hour today," Mrs. C says to me. "Corrine's not feeling well."

She practically snatches the board from me, but I ignore her and begin the tiptoe down Corrine's hall, careful not to call attention to myself with loud thwacks of my boot heels on the floor. Sounds of muffled coughing drift past the half-opened doors, and all the closed ones are shut tight and way too quiet. I inhale quick so as not to swallow the full stench of urine, Clorox, and meatloaf smells that hang in the air, but it's too late and they're already hovering behind my eyes like a gray cloud. I take my steps slowly, nodding at a moon-faced orderly who grunts in recognition that I'm here. At Corrine's door I knock, exhaling and relaxing a little. Lately she hasn't answered, so I push on in.

Corrine Shad's one of the few people who ever smile at me when I come into a room. Usually she's perched by the window, flipping through her latest Enquirer for any new weirdness on the planet, and she'll look up and give me this half-grin that only two strokes will allow. But today she's cocooned in her bed, the sheets pulled under her chin, blinking at me like I'm unfocused or fading away.

"Didn't think you'd come," she says, turning a little toward me. "I thought for sure you were sick of me."

"Nah," I say, suddenly feeling giant next to her frail body. The room seems smaller too—and grayer. I step closer and see how blanched her face is, how saggy and old.

"Read the letter that came from my Mimi today," Corrine says, pointing toward the night table next to her bed. "She's probably giving me an update on the kids."

"Okay," I say, reaching for the letter and opening it, trying to hide my arm from Corrine's razor gaze. I've been coming here every week for three months and she never misses a beat with me. Can tell if I'm lying, or if I've been crying, or if I'm high, which was only once.

"Becca," she says, coughing this terrible raggedy cough and trying to pull herself up. "Before you read, I want to talk to you."

"No lecture today, Ms. Shad." I say, turning the letter in my hands. "Everything is fine. I'm going to school, making a few B's, keeping it straight."

She looks at me then, right through me, her clayey gray eyes stone-serious and seeing everything I don't want to show. For a split second she takes me all in—my whole body—and rests those eyes briefly on my arm. And I know what she's gonna say next, though with Corrine it could be anything. [Carlyn]

"The doctor came wanderin' in here today, said there's something in my boob."

Her boob? I put the letter down. I thought she was going to tsk tsk my new blue hair, comment on the smell of cigarette smoke in my clothes, comment on my silver-spiked black-leather dog collar—which she says gives her the willies—or comment on the few new scores I've kept on my arm. But now there's this. I see in the creases of her face and unsteady hands something I've never seen on Ms. Shad before—fear. I know I should say something, but for once I don't have anything to say.

"It's cancer, and I guess it's everywhere. . . . But it started in my boob."

She's got her hand on the front of her house-dress. She seems surprised these words come from her own mouth. A lightning flash out the window punctuates her sentence.

"I didn't even know I had any boob left."

I manage a weak smile. My first in weeks. But all I wanna do is smoke.

"Our lives are so short."

I knew this was coming. Her eyes now rest on my arm, which I quickly move from her gaze, grabbing Mimi's letter, opening it with the nose of a ballpoint pen.

"Let's see what we got here," I say, pulling up a chair and pulling down my sleeve so that the elastic around the wrist envelops my thumb, catches there, locks.

"Mama," the letter says, "Seattle is already cold and wet, the summer gone. The corn I planted hasn't matured enough to yield even one cob, but we managed to get a few carrots and beets. I'm sure this rain will manage to rot them in the ground if I don't get them up tomorrow. The onions look good."

Mimi's penmanship looks like a chain of bubbles, and it's hard and slow to read.

"Little Jake is now in T-ball, and Melissa just graduated from the 5th grade."

"Graduated?" Ms. Shad huffs. "You graduate from high school and college, not fifth grade. . . . I swear, kids today want to make a big deal out of every accomplishment. Next thing you know she'll be graduating from eating all her dinner."

I just keep reading. "We're still planning on coming down next month. I've got some news that I want to tell you in person."

"That's it," I say. "That's all there is."

"Tell me what you were like as girl," Ms. Shad says. "Tell me your first memory."

"I'm only here for an hour today, Corrine," I say.

"Bullshit. I might only have an hour left, girl," she says, forcing herself upright and patting the bedside, inviting me over. "When an old lady asks for something, it's good manners to do what she says. Now get your anorexic ass over here, and tell me a tale."

And though I don't know how to tell a story, I try. Maybe I felt sad for her. Maybe I saw an opportunity to talk and be heard for the first time in my life without a shrink in the room. Maybe I figured it was safe because she was gonna die anyway. Whatever the reason, I told Ms. Shad stuff I didn't know I could tell. Over the next five months with Ms. Shad, before she died, my arms began to itch. But that's what scabs do when they heal, you know. [Carissa]

Eight

Punctuation As Editing

Devan Cook

> The sun, with all those planets revolving around it and dependent upon it, can still ripen a bunch of grapes as if it had nothing else in the universe to do.
>
> —Galileo, from a Celestial Seasonings tea packet

In this essay I focus on ways to use punctuation to revise and improve your writing. Although we rarely think or talk about it, punctuation makes meaning: it tells us how to read texts and, perhaps more importantly, how to structure the ideas in texts as we read. Interaction between the meaning making of words and the meaning making of punctuation helps writers and readers connect. And when they do, the whole is greater than the sum of its seemingly insignificant parts. Like the relationships between Galileo's solar system and ripening grapes in this essay's epigraph, a piece of writing is a complex system; changes in one part of the system affect other parts.

While correctness is expected in polished writing, punctuation is not mostly about correctness: what the punctuation says and how it affects our reading, writing, and understanding are much more important and also more useful, as we'll discuss later. A skilled writer with sophisticated punctuation skills—beyond the level of periods, question marks, complete sentences, and commas in the appropriate places—knows how to suggest emphasis, connection, analysis, contrast, definition, explanation, and summary in readers' minds simply by using punctuation.

Just as Galileo's grapes provide silent evidence of the sun's work, punctuation use in an essay bears witness to a writer's skill. Thus, the organic relationship between words and punctuation in a piece of writing can be helpful in revision because looking closely at punctuation allows writers to view their work in radically altered ways: to discover new relationships and possibilities as well as previously undiscovered gaps and holes, and to work from that new knowledge to reorder and expand the text to make it more readable and more satisfying to readers.

I'd like to consider one clarification, one question, and one disclaimer. The clarification concerns ways this chapter talks about revision. Since the chapter is about editing, you may have assumed what's discussed here is later-stage revision, when rethinking and reordering have finished and only tidying up is left: tweaking word choice, omitting redundancies, running spelling and grammar checkers.[1] And in fact we're going to look at the relationship of punctuation and revision, which sounds even more like conventional editing. Get out the red pen and the list of proofreader's marks!

But that's not the way this essay considers editing punctuation. In previous writing classes, you probably focused on getting the punctuation "right," and that was all. This essay is about using punctuation to revise. Learning more about punctuation can prompt you to ask important questions about your draft's meaning, and those questions can lead to more invention, drafting, and reflection. This is what revision really means; the fact that your punctuation should improve as you implement the ideas in this chapter is a nice bonus.

So here we focus on ways of editing punctuation invites us to rethink and reorder a piece of writing. Peter Elbow says even an essay with a lot of what he calls "static" or "fog-like elements" (1998, 131) contains "really decipherable, really meaningful . . . messages. Most of them consist of too many and too conflicting messages which *function* as static because they are only half-coded and not in good order" (131). So using the strategies suggested here to revise your work can help your essays become clear, thorough, well organized, more unified and coherent, and more focused. Paradoxically, they may also sound more like you, an expression of and communication from your best informed and most skilled writing self.

In what follows, using published and student writing, I demonstrate how semicolons suggest a call-and-response or question-and-answer movement or relationship, how colons introduce and emphasize examples or actors, and how dashes can emphasize and open up the essay, too, by bringing in different voices. Then, taking another look at what you're working on, you'll start your punctuation revision with a heuristic—a set of prompting questions—to make sure you in fact have everything you need, and then you'll use the same punctuation to help you rework your essay toward a form that is more active, informative, and dialogic (conversational) as well as more orderly and academically acceptable because your organization, emphasis, and analysis will all be there. And your writing needs these characteristics whether you're writing a personal essay or something more expository such as a political science paper.

Effects Achieved with Punctuation

- Do you want emphasis? Try a dash or a short sentence.

- Do you want connection or contrast (which is a kind of connection)? Use a semicolon.

- Do you want to analyze something? A semicolon or a colon will help you structure the analysis.

1. For a list of activities likely in early-, middle-, and late-stage revision, see Wendy Bishop's *The Subject Is Writing*, 3d edition (2003).

- Do you want to define, explain, or summarize? Try a colon, a dash, or a dash skewer.

These are big claims, but I'm not making them up; in fact, I rely on these strategies, especially when I'm in a hurry or my drafts, despite a lot of work, are still in great need of revision. Here's the disclaimer: the midrange of punctuation, such as semicolons, colons, and dashes, that I discuss here is very complex, and there's a great deal more to be said about it than what I'm saying. When you know how to use a semicolon correctly, it's not difficult. The rules are really pretty simple. But looking at your materials differently, seeing the inherent possibilities, and choosing patterns of punctuation that suggest relationships that seem most appropriate to you in your draft—that's often challenging. It's also revision. So try these ideas, and let me know how they work for you. My email address is *dcook@boisestate.edu*.

Confession 1

I love cinnamon, and because I love it I put it places where other people don't usually: in chili, spaghetti sauce, and along with salt and pepper in flour I shake chicken pieces in before frying. Just a dash. My mom used to put that much in matzo balls for soup; she said cinnamon underlines and balances the other flavors, helps them stand out. We ate her matzo balls slowly, savoring each bite.

I love commas, too, and treated them like cinnamon (as seasoning, pause, emphasis) when I returned to school in 1990 after twenty years away. I was forty-two. A red-pen-wielding professor pointed out this practice wouldn't do. So I had to get a handbook and learn the comma rules. Once I got those, I was forced to learn something about semicolons since they replaced my previous comma splices. In high school I'd learned that a semicolon denoted a pause somewhere between a comma and a period; now I discovered that wasn't all I needed to know about semicolons.

Later I worked as a tutor in a writing center for a punctuation-besotted and brilliant teacher. She loved semicolons almost as much as she loved teaching and students, so she used to do punctuation exercises with us tutors once a month after the writing center had closed. Attendance was compulsory. I did not like participating because I was not confident I could employ semicolons appropriately, although by this time I could recite the MLA comma rules cold and was very proud of myself.

I fear I sound a little sarcastic about both of these teachers, but I do not mean to be. Both were brilliant, rigorous, caring teachers who got my attention, opened my mind, and taught me a great deal; this is not easy to do.

"Devan," said the writing center director. "How would you punctuate the last sentence?" I don't remember the long-ago sentence, but in its absence the sentence ending the paragraph above will work as an example.

I thought. "Put a semicolon between *deal* and *this*," I offered.

"Yes. What else could you use?"

I was stumped. What else? After a lengthy, embarrassing wait, she announced, "A colon! That would be a better choice because the clause that follows explains the first clause in the sentence. Of course a semicolon is correct, but a colon is better." Why, I wondered, why? The handbook wasn't much help.

Nevertheless, I had to write seminar papers and a master's thesis, and as I drafted these pieces I practiced with semicolons and colons so I could help writing center clients use them correctly. By this time I had realized the whole department regarded semicolons with special affection.

As I was printing my master's thesis, I noticed my writing was different than it had been: I was able to discuss complex ideas and connect, compare, and analyze them intelligently. For the first time in my life, my writing showed I knew my subject and could discuss it with comfort and confidence. Convincing my teachers of this fact had been one of my biggest challenges as a student; much of my previous writing was garbled and incoherent, if informed. Now that hurdle was behind me.

I thought about this for several days; I wondered whether following the comma rules and writing with semicolons and colons had made me think in different ways. And I decided that was what had happened. Over time, I have become as intrigued with the meaning-making possibilities inherent in colons and semicolons as the people who taught me were.

What Do I Mean About Punctuation, Exactly?

If I were you, I'd be skeptical about all this: after all, it's easy for me to say. Here's a fine example of what I'm talking about from the popular press. In this excerpt from a newspaper essay titled "Doing Good When You're Doing Well," which discusses the relationship of business and community, Tavis Smiley uses semicolons and colons to make his writing clear and memorable:

> You have to be totally responsive to customers' concerns and demands. Competition is too stiff; if you ignore your public, you won't survive.
>
> I would argue that this is particularly true of minority businesses. Not only do you have to do your job, but it seems to me there's also an undeniable expectation that if you're making money off the community, you owe the community something in return: money, internships, support for civic endeavors. There's a sense of being in it together: "I understand your struggle; you understand mine." And you appreciate the fact that if customers are going to spend their hard-earned dollars at your business, you'd better darn well respect that and give them your best service in return.
>
> I don't think anyone says to Bill Gates, "We buy your software, so you'd better give back to us." Now, don't get me wrong; Gates does that anyway. But there's not the same pressure and responsibility placed on him as is placed on minority business owners. (2003, 16)

This excerpt reveals a clear sense of Smiley's voice; you may not be surprised to learn that he has an hour-long daily program on National Public Radio.

How does he communicate voice in writing, the sense that someone intelligent and thoughtful is talking to us? Looking closely, we can see that while the language he uses is precise and specific, there's no jargon. It's very clear. Most of the sentences are short, whether they raise or emphasize a point: even sentences that employ semicolons are short. There are no wasted words. But they often imply questions or responses: "if you ignore your public, you won't survive" responds to and answers the implied question How can one succeed in business when competition is as stiff as it is? This sentence also summarizes Smiley's message in the essay. The third semicolon introduces a response to a warning: don't misunderstand about Bill Gates' business strategies.

Some of the sentences, like the first one with a colon in the second paragraph quoted, are quite long: they encapsulate information or sum up what the writer has said earlier. These ideas are his lineup or cast of suggestions, which are quite specific: give back to the community with "money, internships, support for civic endeavors." This sentence contains an outline that could be expanded upon in separate paragraphs or sections if Smiley were writing something longer. Having introduced his ideas as characters, he could develop them further if he wished. Reading this piece, I do not find myself wanting to break away or wondering what in the heck he's getting at. Smiley's not a self-indulgent writer. But he is skillful in a way all of us can aspire to emulate.

Semicolons

You may not have thought about it before, but essays such as Smiley's and stories have a lot in common: both genres of writing exist in time, work from a central relationship or conflict, and dramatize by illustrating. And you can save yourself a great deal of time and trouble by making sure that the central relationship or conflict or question and answer of your essay is expressed in a sentence with a semicolon, since in ancient Greece the mark we call a semicolon served as a question mark. There's still that aura of question about it: in "Notes on Punctuation," Lewis Thomas writes, "The semicolon tells you that there is still some question about the preceding full sentence; something needs to be added; it reminds you sometimes of the Greek usage" (1979, 126). We see this relationship quite clearly in "Doing Good When You're Doing Well." Rick Leahy comments, "[T]he semicolon . . . sets up a kind of . . . theme-response relationship between statements" (n.d., 7). When I use *theme* later on in this essay, I mean theme in this musical sense, as *a phrase with meaning that is repeated and played upon* rather than as a *theme* like a topic sentence or a whole composition. A similar way of looking at this relationship is as a call and response, a pattern of discourse in which one person or group says something back to another. Sentences with semicolons, then, will usually involve more than one voice, even if differences between the two voices are muted and subtle. (And it helps to remember that in all its uses, it separates coordinate elements.)

Most academic essaying is inquiry-based, as Bruce Ballenger points out in his textbook *The Curious Researcher* when he writes, "It is the value of *not knowing* that is, partly, at the heart of this book" (2001, xxii). When you think about starting with a question or see your theme as a question, something unresolved that wants a response rather than a flat pronouncement of fact, then you can see how a sentence containing a semicolon will help you state your important questions and responses. This kind of connecting, relating, continuing, or contrasting movement is typical of essays; it's also a large part of what happens in stories.

For example: *Once upon a time in a faraway land a good queen died, and the king remarried so his daughter would not be lonely.*

What's unresolved here?

Well, everything: *The new queen was jealous of her stepdaughter's beauty; she fed Snow White a poisoned apple.*

The Snow White fairy tale is based on the call and response or question and answer contained in those two sentences.

You can use the same strategies to construct your essay's central movement—its wholesome, nonpoisonous core. Deanara, one of my students, uses this approach in a researched essay about alternative medicine when she writes, "Consider this: The nutritional approach is natural; pills are not." In this sentence, "pills are not" both replies to and fulfills or supplements the claim that nutritional treatments are more natural than pharmaceuticals—and this is, in fact, her main claim or thesis in the essay. Like Tavis Smiley, Deanara chooses her words (all ten of them) and punctuation carefully to communicate clearly to readers what she is about.

Lana uses a similar approach as she begins an essay about reality TV: "The mainstream-television-viewing public has become obsessed with 'reality' which strikes me as odd; I've always thought that television was a way to escape the mundane reality of our lives." The first clause states that reality is popular (actually multiple constructs of reality); the second responds that this fact is curious given the escapist nature of television viewing. The rest of the essay plays with and plays out this theme and response regarding the curious concept of reality TV.

Brian, writing about a failed relationship, delivers this memorable list of questions with no answers and a story that can go on and on and on:

> Love is always a mixed bag. It's receiving a valentine for the first time in ten years from a woman who doesn't share your feelings; it's holding her so close and so tightly that you can hear the tears roll down her cheek; it's bulbous breasts with soft, succulent nipples; it's raspberry freckles and almond eyes; it's the lingering taste of rum and coke on her lips and the fading flavor of whipped cream on her thighs; it's following, with your eyes, the entire length of her bare leg to the floor where her toes are curled like a ballerina's against the carpet and thinking it's the most beautiful thing you've ever seen in your life; it's hearing the words "I like you as a friend"; it's sending a bou-

quet of flowers that have already withered from thirst; it's awaiting the results of a biopsy that never took place; it's confessing your feelings and waiting two months for a reply; it's days, weeks, months of no phone calls, no e-mails, no visits, for no reason; it's being assaulted by a hailstorm of maybes while yeses and nos sit on the sidelines and eat popcorn; it's flaxen hair; it's hazy gray silence; it's a peck on the cheek; it's a knee to the crotch; it's a double-faced coin with smiles on one side and vicious fangs on the other; it's robins and blue jays and lilacs and honeysuckle and a shaft of wood with a heart shaped tip being ripped from your chest.

Colons

Most of us come to college with more knowledge about colons than about semi-colons because we know they mean "such as" and are used to introduce lists. What we may not realize is how useful the listing function can be, since colons help us dramatize by illustrating (or unpacking or analyzing or summarizing) reasons for our response to the essay's guiding question, call, or theme (the information the semicolon helps us compose and communicate). A sentence with a colon points out the major areas of specifics in the response. A sentence with a semicolon and a sentence with a colon can summarize a whole essay or one portion of an essay, which can be tremendously valuable to you as a writer: with their use you signal to your teacher and other readers that you have done your research and/or prewriting, drafted and thought thoroughly, and composed your ideas in an easily accessible, reader-friendly format.

In fact, colons have their charms, as Aaron, a river-rafting guide, demonstrates in this sentence describing a campfire conversation with a client (accompanied by the client's single-malt scotch) about salmon recovery: "We go on like this for some time: downing three or four dollars at a time and babbling about dams, 50 lb. fish that no longer exist, hunting, river management, and hallucinations." The colon allows him to offer a thumbnail sketch of the scene and the characters involved while also pointing out the major arguments on either side of the salmon question; the sentence also provides a map of what's to come in the essay, which moves into a more mystical incantation to the fish as the writer realizes how unlikely salmon recovery actually is.

Colons also provide emphasis, although as Lewis Thomas writes, "they give you the feeling of being rather ordered around" (1979, 127). Thomas first published "Notes on Punctuation" in 1974, and since that time colon use has increased tremendously. If you don't believe me, pick up the next issue of *Newsweek* that you see lying around and look for colons in the first few paragraphs of the lead story. The text will probably be peppered with colons; perhaps today people (readers, teachers) are so stressed and distracted that they need to be ordered around a bit.

I know I do. When a student's essay almost screams *"Here are my main points"* with the use of a colon, I confess I am relieved because then I'm sure the student knows what her main points are or what she wants me to notice most, as Jackee does in this excerpt from a tongue-in-cheek essay about Idaho drivers: "Idaho drivers are something safe for me to hate: I hate them for everything their status symbol metal boxes stand for. . . . It feels good to have my petty quarrels, but it feels better to give them some importance: I could be this-week's-person-to-avoid-at-the-grocery-store." The strength of her irritation and her awareness of it come across equally strongly because of her use of colons, which allow her to construct a multifaceted picture of road rage.

Dashes

Like colons, dashes are used more often today than they once were, when they were considered a little too informal for polite company. Email has changed all that, and I who have always loved dashes—they were my first punctuation crush—say hurrah. Dashes can be used as singles or in pairs; whether they are alone or together, dashes emphasize—visually, they're hard to miss—and also, because they disrupt a sentence, they open it up to a different tone or voice. I gave a draft of this essay to one of my classes as optional reading; here's what one class member, Melissa, wrote about dashes in her response to me: "I always felt that the words between dashes screamed 'read what's inside me—it's funny, or naughty, or informative' or a dash at the end hinting that what comes up next is a snide comment, or you should anticipate something: funny, enlightening, shocking, whatever." She's right, of course: and notice how she uses the dash and the colon to emphasize her ideas and offer a summarized analysis of how a dash affects her reading experience.

Nevertheless, sometimes dashes emphasize in a way that seems quite different. What follows a dash or is contained within a pair of them is often something that might be whispered, something you might think but would hesitate to say because you think it's not essential, perhaps, or you're not sure your hearers or readers are the right audience for this information, or for information expressed just this way, in perhaps a more private voice. Breaking this phrase or clause or comment out of the sentence—whispering rather than asserting—causes it to be more noticeable. I have even seen the summary of evidence that traditionally follows a colon enclosed within double dashes, to good effect.

So in the sentence I quoted earlier from Aaron's essay, the important details—expensive whiskey, dams, wishful thinking, and endangered fish populations—could also have been presented in a sentence punctuated like this.

Dashes are chatty, a place to address readers more directly. But they also allow for dialogue within the sentence itself, which gives the reader a sense that he is eavesdropping on a good conversation. This sense of conversation that the use of dashes fosters is an important characteristic of the essay, as Lad Tobin writes: "Essays should reflect the way we think and experience the world. And the fact is, we often think and experience the world in a multidimensional, multivoiced way" (1997, 47). In fact, often the information contained after a dash or within double dashes makes readers feel they are overhearing the writer's thoughts, internal dialogue. Thus, a student describes insomnia: "I lie awake contemplating sleep . . . as my eyes—too weary of remaining closed—move about my room." While she tells readers that she looks around her room while she thinks about sleep, she adds another layer of meaning by explaining, almost as if she were talking to herself, that she's been awake so long she's even tired of keeping her eyes closed. Lewis Thomas explains,

> The dash is a handy device, informal and essentially playful, telling you that you're about to take off on a different tack but still in some way connected with the present course—only you have to remember that the dash is there, and either put a second dash at the end of the notion to let the reader know that he's back on course, or else end the sentence, as here, with a period. (1979, 128)

That sense of conversation between the subject and something connected to the subject engages readers while allowing you as the writer an opportunity to reveal the breadth and depth of your knowledge.

Possible combinations among punctuation choices are numerous and can achieve a seemingly infinite number of effects. For example, in an essay about the practice of assigning group grades, Cece writes:

> Group projects have the potential to teach many important skills: teamwork, time management, etc. They present each student the benefits of brainstorming, to combine the creative juices of a small number of people. These are all positive. What is not positive—with a group of people with mismatched expectations and abilities—is assigning a grade to each of the individuals in the group that is an average of the grades earned by each member.

Here the colon introduces the list of usually offered reasons for assigning collaborative work, the short sentence lets the reader know that the negatives are coming, and the double dashes contain the points Cece wants to make about why group grading doesn't always work.

You've probably noticed that Tavis Smiley's essay does not use dashes, a choice that allows him to maintain direct address to the reader throughout his brief, focused essay. As Martha Kolln notes, punctuation choices are among those strategies that have effects on readers (2003, 271).

Strategies for Using Punctuation

The idea that using certain kinds of punctuation can help you rethink and therefore improve what you write is a big promise; here are some suggestions for ways you might explore this for yourself:

1. *Collect punctuation.*
You'll quickly see that different publishers and editors choose different punctuation styles. Look for periodicals that use the punctuation marks you're interested in—dashes, semicolons, and colons. Some likely places include *Time,
Newsweek, National Geographic, Canadian Geographic,* and the *New Yorker.*
Note that these are general-interest magazines, nothing fancy. Introductory
paragraphs and conclusions often contain interesting punctuation—these are also
places where sophisticated punctuation can serve *you* well.

2. *Collect punctuation patterns, alternative and otherwise.*
A good usage text, such as Martha Kolln's *Rhetorical Grammar* (2003) or, for
that matter, any handbook, will outline some conventional academic punctuation patterns for you. In some ways, punctuation marks are like road signs;
they tell readers how to read what you've written. We expect a caution sign
before a railroad crossing; that's a common pattern. In introductions to essays,
often you'll find something like this: Sentence containing comma. Short sentence or sentence containing a phrase within double dashes. Sentence with
two independent clauses joined by a semicolon. A second sentence containing
a colon and a list. Short sentence. You might try writing out a few of your paragraphs this way to see what signs you're giving readers.

3. *Using simplified punctuation, rewrite some of the pieces you've collected.*
Try to make them work as well as you can. For this, simply replacing semicolons with commas and coordinating conjunctions probably won't do. You'll
probably have to rearrange sentences, beef up transitions, add introductory
elements, and vary sentence length to avoid choppiness. None of these are bad
things in themselves: in fact, you should think about adding all these techniques
to your revision arsenal since they make your writing more smooth and readable and create flow. (Whatever *flow* may mean. Wendy Bishop once referred
to flow as "ever-mysterious," and for the past ten years I have been trying to
figure out what aspects of writing we describe with this word. At the moment,
I suspect a text could be said to *flow* when the rhythms of the ideas and of the
words are well matched; neither is too fast nor too slow for the material under
discussion.)

4. *Write yourself a brief memo.*
Then write it again, changing the punctuation. What happened to meaning
when the punctuation changed? Speculate. Be specific. This is for you, not your
teacher. So be honest, too.

5. *Rewrite one of your own introductions and/or conclusions.*
As you do this, imitate some of the punctuation you've noticed elsewhere. Then
do a brief freewrite about how the meaning changed, if it did. Just to be honest, many teachers read introductions and conclusions more carefully than
they read the rest of the essays, particularly if that teacher has many students.

So successfully using all-the-bells-and-whistles punctuation there to achieve all-the-bells-and-whistles thinking—demonstrating knowledge, clarity, and the ability to connect ideas—may benefit you most.

6. *Collect and experiment with unusual punctuation.*
Explore further. Some writers use punctuation that's "wrong" or different: Joan Didion comes to mind, as does Lee Smith. What are these writers doing? Why, when they know the rules, do they choose to break them? What effects do they achieve by doing so? Always considering how your audience is likely to react, what effects can you achieve by trying out what they do?

How to Begin

In *Writing Without Teachers*, Peter Elbow (1998) suggests two metaphors for the writing process: growing and cooking. These two aspects of writing may occur at different times or all at once. Writing develops through growing just as any animal or plant would; growing is likely to involve freewriting, and growing your essay may call for research as well. In cooking, two different ideas or aspects or features of a piece of writing relate and interact; cooking essentially means seeing something about the essay in terms of something else. You can use punctuation, which makes meaning without words, to cook your words. But first, I need to tell you the assumptions I'm making. They may or may not apply to you, but they will suggest what you need to do before you preheat the oven.

- *You're already secure with commas and periods.* If you're foggy about sentence boundaries or the four MLA comma rules, work with a good handbook, your campus writing center, and your teacher.

- *You've already involved yourself with growing the essay.* You've researched thoroughly, struggled through freewriting, confusion, and chaos, and sighed with relief as a center of gravity (or a theme or topic or claim) slowly emerged. I'd like to point out here that too little attention to growing is the single biggest obstacle to revision my students face, and that when I ask my students to use the revision-through-punctuation techniques I'm telling you about, frequently before they get too far in the process they realize they need to do more research and/or freewriting. Revision often invites more (and more focused) invention; in the process of writing this essay, I have returned to invention—freewriting and research—daily for the past two weeks. Using punctuation to help you reorder and clarify your work will not allow you to detour around further invention and rethinking. Trying to proceed without this is like trying to make an omelet with no eggs in the refrigerator. It doesn't work, no matter how hard you try.

- *You've played around with the suggested activities for exploring contemporary punctuation.* At least, you have begun to pay enough attention to how punctuation is used in articles you pick up in the library while waiting for other members of your study group or at the doctor's office to tentatively accept my hypotheses: punctuation makes meaning even though it's not a word, and there's a perfectly ordinary punctuation vocabulary that you've taken for granted as a reader but never tried seriously as a writer because you thought it might be too hard.

• *You may or may not know much about the rules governing the use of semicolons, colons, and dashes*; you may have avoided them because you didn't want to seem as though you didn't know what you were doing. And you were right—when I was there (and occasionally I'm still there), I was right, too. Martha Kolln, the doyenne of American rhetorical grammarians, writes, "Make no mistake, it is important to follow the conventions of punctuation; the effectiveness of your prose diminishes with every error the reader notices" (2003, 84). How true. But you can learn.

• *You'd rather talk about meanings than rules.* As would I.

Confession 2

Another confession: Now that I'm a teacher and most of what I read is student writing, I look for clues to help me predict my reading experience. That is, I look at texts before I read the words. This rests my eyes and saves time; it also allows me to begin organizing and assessing the text in my mind before I read a word of the final draft. Here's what I do: I read the title. If the essay in question is researched, I turn to the works cited page. I read that mostly for interest: what has the writer referred to that I might like to read? This semester students have interested me in a Renaissance physician named Andreas Vesalius and also in rereading Naomi Wolf's *Beauty Myth*: in case you have wondered, we teachers are often engaged by our students' thinking. The works cited list can also allow me to critically evaluate sources—did the student challenge herself and pick up the *Journal of Clinical Psychology* or show a sense of being an informed generalist by citing sources like the *Economist* or *New York Times*, or did she stick with Ask Jeeves or People.com? Before I read the essay, do I look forward with eager anticipation or brace myself for a rough time? If you have noted anxiety and self-protectiveness in my checking of references, you are correct. And of course I look for correctness, but checking for correctness is not my major goal when I first turn to the list of works cited. Later on, after I've actually read the essay, I'll look more closely with correctness in mind and connect the works cited entries with the in-text citations. Finally, I look at the punctuation of the entire piece and the presentation on the page.

Last semester I read a master's thesis that was like a bramble thicket. It made my eyes hurt. It made my brain hurt. Reading it tormented me. It was quite good—critically informed and closely argued—but I had a terrible time untangling the wonderful ideas it contained. It was difficult to sort out what the writer wanted to emphasize, contrast, and connect. Some of the essay's scaf-folding was there in titles and transitions. Some of it was missing. This was problematic because the subject—service-learning pedagogy in first year writ-ing—is not something I know much about. The thesis was formatted in single-spaced Arial font. It was submitted electronically. Paragraphs were long, sometimes a page or more. The punctuation consisted of periods and commas. In the entire sixty-eight pages there were fewer than a dozen semicolons and colons. I noticed this because I don't usually have so much difficulty reading a thesis, and I began to wonder why this thesis was different. During defense, I asked the writer why she had used so few semicolons and colons. I felt fool-ish, a nitpicker, to ask her about punctuation.

"Oh," she said, "I took most of them out because I thought I was using too many." This student was a skilled academic and technical writer; technical writ-ing employs simplified punctuation because its goal is to communicate and per-suade in a straightforward way (I am grossly oversimplifying here), while writing in the humanities aims to explore, unpack, try out and try on, balance, and compare ideas and perspectives. You can do the same things limiting your-self to periods and commas, but it's a lot harder.

(And if you'd like to try, I suggest that you use a font with serifs like Times New Roman, double space, vary sentence length, pay special attention to tran-sitions and introductory phrases and clauses within sentences, and paragraph with great care.)

Writing Like a Reader:
Using Punctuation Options to Revise

First, read back over your draft; read aloud if possible, so you can read slowly and carefully. You want to pay careful attention to what your draft says rather than what you hope it is saying. Remember, these strategies will help, but they will not do the writing for you.

Then get out some paper, set up columns, and make lists. Not all of the lists asked for may apply to your essay, which is fine. But think about each one before moving on.

- List your questions, actual or implied. List all of them. What did you wonder about before you started writing? What inquiry has guided your work?

- List your themes (remember, theme is used in the musical sense), calls, unresolved issues.

- List your focusing point(s), central tension(s), conflict(s), or relation-ship(s).

- Don't edit these lists; jot down whatever you can that seems at least marginally related to a question, theme, hypothesis, or assumption. In each column, star or underline the one that seems most central or important; check the ones that best support that one.

- If you can't identify a most important question or have trouble listing your assumptions, this is a clear indication that you need more growth: freewriting, research, or both.

- If the questions, themes, or focusing points don't seem quite right or important enough to you, start another column: "Questions and assumptions I would write now."

- List your responses to the questions or themes in your draft. Even though you're writing to discover or inquire, by no means does your essay have to contain "answers." A response to a theme or a question does not have to be an answer, although an answer is one kind of response. A response is something said back: that's all. Your responses may be better questions or areas for further exploration or different ways of looking at your beginning question or assumption. Just list your responses.

- If your listed responses don't satisfy you or don't seem to match up with your questions, start another column: "Things I wish I'd said back but didn't."

- List reasons for your responses: what's involved or who, what you want to discuss, your cast of characters or issues. This list should probably contain what you think of as your main points.

- List things you'd like to emphasize or confide to readers that are connected to your questions or claims but aren't listed already.

- On another sheet of paper, make a cluster with your central question or theme and its response(s) at the center. Using the lists of subordinate questions, responses, and related material you'd like to emphasize, explore relationships and connections or conflicts between what's in the lists.

Example 1

I've been revising an essay called "Things to Write With": it's a literacy history or writing autobiography, probably similar to some assignments you've had or will have. Mine is about writing as a way to move between personal history and my public self or roles, and how those transitions have led me to value teaching. Here are the lists I'm working with:

Focusing Points	Relationships	Central Tensions/Conflicts
My writing history	Mom and me	My writing and Mom's
Things to write with (legal pads, pens, etc.)	Mom and her family	Personal ↔ public writing
Mom's writing history	Mom and Dad	Gender roles and writing
Mom's family as writers	Reading and writing	Writing and culture
Dad's desk	Teaching and writing	Mother-daughter conflict

- Draft an introductory paragraph or two: Write a sentence containing a semicolon with your central question or theme with its response(s).

Write a sentence with a colon listing reasons for responses or your main points. Emphasize and establish voice with dashes. This paragraph or two will serve as a blueprint for your essay, for you and for your readers.

Example 2
When I read back over these lists, I can underline the most important elements—what I want to write about; checking off supporting points prompts me to be thorough without allowing a supporting point to take over the essay.

Focusing Points	*Relationships*	*Central Tensions/Conflicts*
✔My writing history	✔Mom and me	My writing and Mom's
✔Things to write with (legal pads, pens, etc.)	✔Mom and her family	✔Personal ↔ Public writing
✔Mom's writing history	Mom and Dad	✔Gender roles and writing
Mom's family as writers	✔Reading and writing	✔Writing and culture
Dad's desk	Teaching and writing	Mother-daughter conflict
Personal ↔ public writing		

As you can see, in the essay for this book, I have used a lot of semicolons to demonstrate connection and conflict, just as check marks, underlining, and the arrows do in this chart.

• Using the blueprint paragraphs as a guide, reorder chunks of your earlier draft.

As a Result . . .

Going through this exercise may require you to tear your essay down and rebuild it from the ground up; it may point out a few spots that need some attention; or it may convince you that you've done a great job and constructed a clear, readable essay that employs the kinds of organization, analysis, and emphasis academic readers (and all readers) expect. (After I've been reading essays for several hours, I crave them.) As you continue to notice ways punctuation is used in essays you read and write, you'll see how punctuation roughs out a scaffold you can build your essays on.

Although this piece has focused on punctuation as a strategy for academic revision, popular and literary writing frequently involves interesting punctuation choices that you can experiment with when you write short stories, op-ed pieces or letters to the editor, or even poems. For example, you may hear in a workshop that poems should not contain semicolons, but they do: Lewis Thomas writes at length about semicolons in T. S. Eliot's "Four Quartets," and Eliot probably knew as much or more about writing poetry than the people in your workshop. As you work with punctuation in several genres, you'll develop a sense of the nuances of a semicolon and also a sense of its usefulness. Rather than taking my word for it, you'll know for yourself. While this is helpful any-time, it is especially good to be skilled at this kind of construction when you are writing or revising in a hurry—which you may be, right now. In either case, good luck!

Thanks to Deanara, Lana, Brian, Aaron, Jackee, Melissa, and Cece for their wonderful writing, some of which is quoted here.

Works Cited

Ballenger, Bruce. 2001. *The Curious Researcher*. 3d ed. Boston: Allyn and Bacon.

Bishop, Wendy. 1999. "Hint Sheet F: A Discussion of Drafting Levels." In *The Subject Is Writing*, 3d ed., ed. Wendy Bishop, 254–55. Portsmouth, NH: Boynton/Cook.

Elbow, Peter. 1998. *Writing Without Teachers*. 2d ed. New York: Oxford University Press.

Kolln, Martha. 2003. *Rhetorical Grammar: Grammatical Choices, Rhetorical Effects*. 4th ed. New York: Longman.

Leahy, Rick. No date. "Using Punctuation." Unpublished essay. Boise State University Writing Center handout.

Smiley, Tavis. 2003. "Doing Good When You're Doing Well." *USA Weekend, Idaho Statesman* 12 Jan.: 16.

Thomas, Lewis. 1979. "Notes on Punctuation." In *The Medusa and the Snail*, 125–29. New York: Viking.

Tobin, Lad. 1997. "The Case for Double-Voiced Discourse." In *Elements of Alternate Style*, ed. Wendy Bishop, 44–53. Portsmouth, NH: Boynton/Cook.

Appendix

Using Punctuation to Revise

This essay suggests that you use punctuation in ways you may have never considered before, as ways to make meaning; if you use these strategies, you'll find yourself writing in ways that may seem unfamiliar. When you think about it, that's the whole point. Nevertheless, here are some pointers you may find helpful:

1. *Expect to use more punctuation than you're accustomed to.* Don't worry: we're not going to run out. And I've never known a teacher who rations semicolons or colons, although there are some who ration dashes.

2. *Try using at least one semicolon, colon, and dash or set of dashes in each paragraph.* Doing so will invite you to organize each paragraph in new ways and to think about connections and contrasts between ideas differently.

3. *Try removing all punctuation other than periods and commas.* How do you have to revise to compensate for the absence of semicolons, colons, dashes?

4. *Now that you've played around with this punctuation for a while, look in some handbooks for the rules.* You'll understand better what you read there, since you now have some experience with colons, semicolons, and dashes. And it's likely that the handbooks will suggest some strategies you'll want to try.

5. *Try writing your own rules.* Realize that these will be a work in progress; usages can differ, evolve, and still be correct—which you always want.

6. *As you continue using colons, semicolons, and dashes, you'll feel more comfortable with them.* A wonderful chef who has a radio program here in Boise, Joyce Doughty, talks about how different the experience of making a hundred fettucine dinners a night is from making fettucine for the family once a month; she says she never really knew how to cook until she opened a restaurant.

Nine

The Case of Creative Nonfiction: Retouching Life

Wendy Bishop

> The writer of any work, and particularly any nonfiction work, must
> decide two crucial points: what to put in and what to leave out.
>
> —Annie Dillard

> You must change your life.
>
> —Rainer Maria Rilke

Having written on request through the years of our schooling, most of us are fairly
proficient with certain types of nonfiction: We've engaged with primary sources,
as when we visit a state park and interview a biologist; we've consulted secondary sources, such as books, maps, magazines, movies, journals, documents from
the library, bookstore, and Internet on the history of the U.S. park system. We've
written to show knowledge, to critique, to argue, and to investigate.

Perhaps you've had the opportunity as well to explore and reflect, to allow
readers to resonate to your particular way of seeing the wide world, to share
your angle of vision, to compose literary essays, what we've taken more
recently to calling *creative nonfiction*. In one sense, any act of composing is
creative if you move from *assigned* writing to *invested* writing, that is, if you
view a subject or a project as your own. In this sort of prose, writers take advantage of the many tools of all literary writing: image, language choices,
metaphor, narrative, and many other techniques.

Indeed, there are subcategories galore within this area. I expect you've
developed preferences about where you situate yourself in nonfiction's many
creative subgenres: literary journalism; travel and nature writing; personal,
persuasive, lyric, and critical essays, to name but a few. Some of us gravitate
toward authors who share complicated factual materials in an elegant and eru-
dite style. Some appreciate detailed arguments. Some look to writers to take
them where they haven't been before, sharing adventures in other countries and
interactions with other cultures. And some of us are drawn to authors pre-

cisely because they don't tell "the facts ma'am, just the facts." Some readers prefer to explore, reflect, and meditate side by side with an author as that writer's narrative unfolds like origami in reverse.

In order to connect with lived experience and shape the far or recent past into new stories, what do authors of nonfiction do, and how do they do it?

What can you learn as they touch and retouch, work and rework, both their lives and their prose through drafting and revision?

Such questions are the focus of this chapter.

Choosing Your Genre:
The Case for (Creative) Nonfiction ·

Authors of nonfiction produce texts that are tentative, investigative, associative, brash, bawdy, subtle, logical, sad, celebratory, angry, and sometimes all these or other things simultaneously. These writers and their readers join Annie Dillard in celebrating a genre, ". . . literary nonfiction [that] is all over the map and has been for three hundred years. There's nothing you can't do with it. No subject matter is forbidden, no structure is proscribed. You get to make up your own form every time" (2002, 244). Even so, it is useful to question the genre's supposed freedoms and seeming formlessness. If you don't, how will you measure your success, the end result of excellent revisions?

Your authorial aims and how well you meet those aims matter, particularly as you begin to draft. Then, the choices you make as you transition from exploring a topic for yourself to sharing it with an interested reader become paramount. In both instances, the choices are many. For example, writers eager to address environmental issues can do so as an argument over opening the Alaskan Wildlife Refuge to oil drilling; can share a terse, data-filled press report with main information in the opening paragraph; can draw a cautionary tale about national hubris and legislators' gamesmanship; may detail a blunt account of dissimilar cultures—Vuntut Gwich'in, Inupiaq, Anglo—perhaps modeled on a Tennessee Williams tragedy; may dramatize one life, that of the author who lit out for the territories, took a job in untamed game-rich oil country, and now hopes to re-create for readers just what it felt like, *back then*. Each of these writers will create different types of creative nonfiction but engage in the same initial processes of developing, evaluating, and revising their text. During the revision process, authors continue to complicate their discussion but begin, as well, to focus and shape subjects to meet personal writing aims.

To have aims, writers need attitudes toward final products. Fiction—things as we imagine them. Nonfiction—things that are not as we imagine them? Things that aren't made up? Posed this way, nonfiction prose seems like leftovers, as if we write about the material we find lying around, easy to come by, factual and uncreative, as if we have nothing to add to lived experience. If you hold beliefs along such lines or if you believe that truth is out there to find, shake off, and set down plainly on the page, you're thinking of a different sort of writing than I am in this chapter. Here I'm speaking to those who believe that who we are and the communities we align ourselves with can't help but influence and color our interpretation of fact and influence our representations of reality. While we don't make it all up when we write creative nonfiction, we certainly filter our prose through our own experience and understanding. We review, we retouch, we interpret.

In this sense, our narratives, like our lives, are always under revision. You and your significant other tell the story of first meeting: two stories. You and your parents recall your seventh-grade soccer game: three stories. You and your roommates review your positions on the 2003 U.S.-Iraq conflict: multiple, complex, contradictory, competing stories. Luckily, nonfiction provides a location for scrutiny and testimony both.

Contending with Relationships Between Fact and Fiction

I argue that any genre is as creative as the author who undertakes to write it. The differences between fiction and nonfiction as genres—types of writing—are clear only at the far ranges of a blended continuum and are increasingly more complicated the closer they come to each other.

Nonfiction	→←—	Fact/Fiction	→←—	Fiction
Very Factual		Proportion Depends on Beliefs and Aims		Very Fabricated

Have you ever read science fiction that wasn't based to some degree on what humans know about gravity, our solar system, and physics? Inventing an inhabited planet with six moons that can be reached by space-traveling humans still requires a grounding in gravity and other subjects. Equally, planet Earth has always—in the documented historical record—had one moon. At least for our lifetimes, this will be fact, based on the triangulation (agreement) of several reliable sources—the image we perceive through a telescope, museum evidence from NASA moon walks, and research data found in books in the campus library. One moon and we trust that we can document it.

Not surprisingly, what you know about fiction will help when you write creative nonfiction (the reverse is also true); authors in both genres use many of the same tools—telling detail, characters, dialogue, narrative, and common organizational structures. Ray Bradbury offers a very humanized view of Martians, and Ptolemy convinces those around him that Earth is the center of the universe—that is, until Copernicus' 1543 "De Revolutionibus Orbium Coelestium" rocked the world. Bradbury builds a world based on the facts of this one; Ptolemy builds a logical explanation for an observed phenomenon, a model, a theory that exists until further knowledge disproves it. Both men created fact-based fictions, one intentionally, one because he had incomplete data. This is why readers look to the author's claims for her text. Scott Russell Sanders feels that "The essay is distinguished from the short story, not by the presence or absence of literary devices, not by tone or theme or subject, but by the writer's stance toward the material" (2002, 336). This is why I emphasize that your intentions (not always met, but intended) and how you signal them to your reader are crucial; it may take you a number of drafts shared with many readers to ascertain what you want to accomplish and whether you've done it successfully.

To Fill or Not to Fill (the Gaps): Thinking Through Truth and Memory

Some authors of nonfiction intentionally take liberty with their subjects by filling in gaps, offering information they couldn't have collected firsthand. Norman Mailer, for instance, wrote *The Executioner's Song*, novel-feeling journalism based on the life of Gary Gilmore. Mailer, a novelist and reporter, clearly mixed his types of expertise in this fused format. Some readers feel used, however, when such a decision isn't made clear, as when an author writes artfully and successfully about his grandparent who died recently when the grandparent is still living or who researches a trip to Mexico and presents it as if it happened, having never left her computer desk. For some readers, creative nonfiction *must have happened*, for others, what matters most is that the report *feels as if it happened*. The second set of readers will tell you they admire a writer who can create a true-feeling narrative and craft it believably; the first set of readers finds this sort of practice abhorrent and unethical.

Fern Kupfer maintains that there are three kinds of lies that are valid when writing creative nonfiction, and each suggests different relationships to revision. Kupfer feels authors may tell white lies. I did this when I couldn't recall the style of my mother's apron in 1958 but knew she wore one. I looked through magazine archives for *Look* and *Life* and watched a sequence of *I Love Lucy* for ideas, then revised using these aids, providing her with a knee-length, ruffle-edged, flower-print apron that tied in the back.

Kupfer identifies a second necessary lie, that of narrative structure. This may take place when the author creates composite characters, compresses time, and/or omits details. For instance, a former boyfriend and I traveled across the Sahara together in 1980 and each of us has since written about that experience. Without consulting the other until years later, we each chose to leave the other out of the narrative in order to make our text less complicated and, we hope, more effective. In an early draft about crossing the Sahara, I struggled to explain my feelings as well as his, until, during revision, I realized I needed one character less to avoid confusion and strengthen the focus.

Kupfer calls the third lie the "the gift of perhaps" (2002, 292–93). In this instance, the writer makes a reasonable guess about how it might have been, is, or will be. Peter Ives reminds us that this gift is an ancient one: "As Aristotle wrote in his *Poetics*: 'It is not the poet's function to describe what actually happened, but the kind of things that might happen, that is, that could happen because they are, in the circumstances, either probable or necessary . . .'" (2002, 273). To revise, the writer asks "What if?" and answers it several different ways until he arrives at the one response that feels most true, most necessary, to accurately shape the narrative. We see this in *The Executioner's Song, In Cold Blood,* and many other imaginative fact-based texts.

If you begin revising the truth the moment you decide to write about an event, each draft moving you toward a more substantial text, how do you now decide which "truth" prevails or whether a composite truth is the best arrangement? A basic suggestion is that you will want, lifelong, to interrogate your own beliefs about the relationships of fact to fiction and memory to truth. And be aware that creative nonfiction may change your experiences permanently: Mary Clearman Blew claims that whatever truth you report in your prose will now become the one you remember, lifelong, altering and solidifying earlier impressions into the narrative you decide to construct (2002, 234).

Even so, the difficulty you have knowing if you're informing fact with a little fiction or creating fiction based on facts that you've taken (great) liberties with is only your first decision, often one that's made for you by the assignment. It is equally challenging to find the best structure for your piece, to decide, finally, what to put in and what to leave out, as you return to your drafts, a necessity pointed out by Annie Dillard in the quote that opens this chapter. However, if you've used your first draft to explore—recklessly, fully, deeply—because "a careful first draft is a failed first draft" (Hampl 2002, 263), you're poised now to answer "What next?" The eight suggestions that follow should provide some directions to consider as you proceed.

Looking for Revision in All the Right Places

1. *Explore the proportions and relationship of fact to fiction in your text.*
Many writers take the same influential life episode and cast it in several genres across their writing lifetime. "It has been my experience," Peter Ives explains, "that we do not perceive or write about things as they are, but rather, we perceive or write about them as *we* are" (2002, 275). You may find out more about who you are in relation to your material if you examine a story, scene, or incident in more than one format.

Try This

Tell the same story, scene, or incident as a fact-based narrative and as a piece of fiction. Begin with an essay and then rewrite the essay as fiction or begin with fiction and then write the essay that illuminates the factual events behind your fabrication.

> I was drunk on sake the night I came home to my mother's message in late May. It had already been a bad night. My girlfriend, Kim, had broken up with

me on my porch after a tense meal of fried rice and Chinese wine and driven away with a dramatic screech of her car wheels. I was sitting on my couch, unsure of what to do with myself when I noticed the blinking red light of the answering machine. "Call home" was all my mother said. I dialed the numbers just as Jennifer walked in smiling and ready to go to Grand Finale's, our usual Thursday night haunt.
—from Carmela Starace's nonfiction "Night Time Elegy" (2003, 432)

The day had started without distinction. Another sunny May day in her hidden cottage that Regina rented for almost nothing. She had made Rice-a-Roni for breakfast, driven her neighbor—a lesbian pagan witch from West Virginia—to a doctor's appointment, and returned an overdue movie to Blockbuster. Later, she and Kim went out for Sushi and ended up on Regina's front porch arguing. Kim was being stifled, she said. She needed time for herself. Regina had been saddened but not surprised. She knew when they had first dated that Kim wasn't a one-woman kind of girl. To Kim's credit, she'd tried. Six months had passed without even a roving eye, but Regina had seen it building up lately. So while Kim cried and apologized, Regina held her and told her it would be okay. Kim left quickly, reminding Regina how she loved her and Regina sat on the porch for a long time, hearing the phone ring again and again but not wanting to answer it.
—Carmela Starace's fiction "Black Dress, White Polka-Dots," printed with "Night Time Elegy" (2003, 436)

In these drafts, Carmela changes from a first- to a third-person narrator as she moves from fact to fiction. In her essay, she briefly mentions her sexual orientation, whereas she uses the fictional text to explore the relationship between the narrator, Regina, and her girlfriend, Kim (who, interestingly, is named Kim in both genres), more fully. While the essay emphasizes action, the fictional account captures the event in a more leisurely and cinematic manner. In both, Carmela's aim is to share her feelings about her brother's unexpected death. She'll need to decide which text does this best and which is more comfortable for her to write. To decide, she'll share her drafts with readers and evaluate their responses.

2. Consider authorial presence.
When Carmela changes point of view, you, as reader, are taken farther away from her subject. First- (*I*), second- (*you*), and third-person (*he, she, it*) points of view are available to authors in both genres, but authors generally agree that no matter which point of view is chosen and which genre, the narrator is always a construct: "The first person singular," explains Scott Russell Sanders, "is too narrow a gate for the whole writer to squeeze through. What we meet on the page is not the flesh-and-blood author, but a simulacrum, a character who wears the label *I*" (2002, 336). In fact, when you think of your factional self as a character, you can more readily develop a useful, critical distance from

your essay. There is nothing inherently close or distant about any point of view; more telling is how much of the first-person singular you squeeze into your text and where that decision places your reader and narrator in relation to the action.

Try This

Write a story in first person and then try a second-person or third-person version (or both).

> I had expected her to look like a gypsy, I guess. I had found out about her from Sissy, a friend of mine: Libby Clark, a visiting spiritualist medium from England, in Tallahassee to give a public reading at the Unity Church on a Thursday evening in May. I suppose I should have had Jonathan Edwards in mind, the quite normal-looking guy on television, calmly and oh, so credibly relaying messages to people in his audience sitting on black platforms like bleachers. He wears Docker-like pants and sweaters.
> —Sandra, from the first draft of her essay on mediums, titled "The Medium"
>
> On a Thursday evening in May in Tallahassee, Florida, Libby Clark, a medium from England, spoke at the Unity church on Crowder Road, near the Indian Mounds. At ten minutes past the announced starting time, the audience was as big as it was going to get, less than fifty people, mostly middle-aged, except for the three teenagers toward the back of the crowd, which was actually the middle of the room. Marilyn ____, head of the Tallahassee chapter of the Foundation for Spiritual Knowledge, introduced her, and she walked down the center aisle toward the stage from the back. She was forty-ish with blonde-colored hair, wearing a knee-length sleeveless lavender dress. She looked like someone who would be seen working at a department store in the mall. Or someone in church. As she walked, the tail of her lavender scarf floated behind her like a silky, diaphanous cloud, but she walked like she was ready to get to the stage and begin, like her feet touched the ground firmly.
> —Sandra's new opening to "The Medium," now titled "The Mediums, Their Message"

In the first draft, the reader is situated as someone overhearing the writer's narration: "I had, I had, I should." In the second, the reader is more clearly being presented with the character of Libby Clark, the medium. In the first draft, the narrator is central, in the second, the focus shifts to the entrance of Libby and her lavender scarf.

3. Consider the problems and processes of memory.
Access your material by all available means. As you start a memoir or a personal reflection, you may be hampered by the feeling that it's too late: X is dead and you're too far from the people who once knew him to do a good job of re-creating what it felt like that summer long ago with him, or you haven't seen

him for ten long years; you've forgotten so much. Perhaps, or perhaps not. Explore a variety of memory triggers. "What transports me back to the past varies greatly: sometimes it's the way my son drops his head when I'm angry; sometimes it's an old Beatles song, a photo album, or a receipt I found in the pocket of a coat I haven't worn in years" (Ives 2002, 272). Like Peter Ives, listen to music, watch relatives, look at photos. Attempt to activate involuntary memory:

> Voluntary memory is the memory of multiplication tables, bus schedules, and daily agendas—memories that we intellectually attempt to provoke. Involuntary memory, on the other hand, occurs when a recollection is stirred by "a long forgotten smell or an old glove." Something that has remained dormant since childhood and "therefore remains uncorrupted by later associations." These instances of almost epiphanic intensity are also known as *Proustian moments.* (Ives 2002, 272)

Before you know it, you'll remember that one cousin has your uncle's nose, recall your grandmother's habit of rubbing her left cheek when worried, and so on. Your research can also take you back: consult family and friends, but also "reread" those times. Find a magazine, look at the ads, read newspaper headlines, learn more about the world events that would have absorbed these individuals' attention and energy (think of how screenwriters did this to develop *That Seventies Show*). Doing so can help you (re-)create time, place, and people in your drafts. If you're lucky, a crucial player in the story will still be alive, available to you by visit, phone, or Internet. This person is worth contacting because someone who shared your voluntary memories can often trigger involuntary ones as well. Just don't expect her to agree on the facts.

Try This

1. After mapping out the general time/place/persons/events you hope to explore, collect some triggers that vault you intentionally into involuntary memory, Proustian time. Search to re-create an ephiphanic moment. Open a photo album. Play music. Return to your hometown. Listen to old tunes. Play a tape of a family member talking. Watch old family videos or movies from that time period. Get more active still: eat your favorite childhood comfort foods, shop vintage stores to find that madras sports coat your relative wore. As you work actively to access your involuntary memories, be sure to freewrite, photograph, tape, and take notes. You'll want to review these later.

2. Write down everything you remember about an individual in your narrative. (Treat him like a character: what does he always say, wear, work at? Create a narrative resume: list hobbies, cars owned, towns visited, friends, family members, and so on.) Then, if possible, conduct an interview with that individual to help you better represent him, to collect

details, to recuperate and/or correct your memories. If necessary, research the popular culture of the time in which your essay takes place as in exercise 1 above. Expect each draft to benefit by a repeat of these activities. Dig deep.

I already knew Mila before I got started, so when I went to "interview" her I did not have enough distance to stage the "scene" in the coffee shop. We interviewed, again, and I got more info, but not enough. For the final draft, I drove out to Asheville or Monticello or wherever she lives (off the Upper Aucilla River) and stayed an entire day with her and her husband. I found/find Mila interesting as both a wife and a scholar, and as a woman. What slant to take?! I collected the stories and blended them as best I could, in something that flows but is not too structured.
—Amanda, from her process memo for "By the Difficult Things"

The general story of my birth was about the same coming from both my mom and my dad. But, they each remembered specific details that the other did not. Between the two of them, I gathered the most vivid description of my birth and the weather that surrounded it.
—Rachel, on her essay "Blizzard Baby"

The trouble I had with this piece was immense. I'll go ahead and tell you that you're right about my poor choice of subject. Well, not poor exactly, but probably not wise. I should have been there to observe, but I really thought I could pull it off [recall Fay Knighton without revisiting her]. . . .
—Jay, process narrative for "Songs in the Key of Fay"

Amanda reminds us that we need, at times, to conduct interviews in unfamiliar locations in order to (re)see a familiar individual or to place her in her own territory. Rachel realized that the more sources she consulted, the better would be her re-creation, so she consulted both parents and newspaper weather reports from the year she was born. And Jay admitted that the confusions readers had deciphering his aims resulted from his reliance on an old interview. Returning to a draft several years after the original talk only by looking at his notes and consulting his memory (instead of attempting a second interview), he failed to make the new draft vivid and clear to his readers.

4. *Consider the way humans rely on recurring patterns and archetypes to understand the world.*
Honor your learning, get help from all you've read and seen and done. Find a mentor, a coach, someone or some text to emulate. That's regularly how we learn: language, sports, the arts. Others have done this before you. *Once upon a time* and *happily ever after* and *it was a dark and stormy night* and *the good guys always win* are dependable structures within which any of us can explore our experiences. And those expected structures are particularly striking when we ring changes upon them or reverse them, when the ending isn't happy or the

bad guys win or the narrator lets us see that the mean stepmother actually had her reasons. This is because readers come to texts with genre expectations (mystery writers do this, they don't do that) that writers trigger, and readers expect to have their genre expectations met . . . or to know why they aren't. (See Chapter 5 for advice on revising to push on and explore genre expectations.)

Narrative structures also let us understand events that we formerly didn't: they are lenses for examining a subject. As we age and have our own children, we better understand how the loss of a child or a betrayal by spouse could completely change a life. Joan Didion suggests that "we live entirely, especially if we are writers, by the imposition of a narrative line upon disparate images, by the 'ideas' with which we have learned to freeze the shifting phantasmagoria which is our actual experience" (quoted in Sanders 2002, 330). For many, nonfiction appeals because nonfiction allows them to create new meaning and enables both writer and readers to freeze experience long enough to help them learn from and appreciate an event.

Try This

Borrow a structure to help you (re)organize your narrative. Use the diary form or letter form to allow you to (re)tell the story. Your memoir might echo a Shakespearean comedy or tragedy (fiction writers do this often; Jane Smiley's a *Thousand Acres* revises *King Lear*). Perhaps you'll choose to follow the classic "coming of age (as an artist)" story by composing a bildungsroman or kunstleroman, respectively; most writers can't resist this subject at some point in their career. You can also appropriate the rules: use school patterns of development (comparison, contrast, cause and effect, and so on) playfully. Use these to structure personal, lyrical essays in ways that call attention to the forms and the ways those forms deliver one version out of many that could be shared. In "It's Not the Heat, It's the Humidity," I used form as a trigger for a comparison I wanted to develop:

> This is my first and last five-paragraph, comparison and contrast essay. With a few twists, the twist of key-lime in a Florida gin and tonic, the twist of an ankle on ice outside the front door in Alaska, and the twist that I'm a Californian in a continuous state of displacement. Just as everyone else drifted toward California—over-pricing the real-estate and bankrupting the public schools—I went the other way, north, then south. I'm composed of California's irreproducible coastal mornings, light fog burning off into even-handed Mediterranean afternoons on patios with potted red geraniums. I never saw snow until I was eighteen—this on a church-camp snow trip—and I never saw snow *falling* until a year after that in a square in Salzburg during the gray unfamiliar gloom of a real fall afternoon. Then again, I never felt true tropical heat and persistent humidity until my Uncle Bill sent my girlfriend JoAnn and me on a cruise to the Bahamas the year we visited him in Sarasota as college girls. In fact, until six years ago, I never experienced

warm mid-winter storms, hurricane force winds, and Spanish moss flying
through the air like displaced witches' wigs. Now I live in Tallahassee and just
before that in Fairbanks, Alaska, and both seem times of elected service
abroad, across land and landscapes, into and out of cultures and climates—
meeting Athabascans and Apalachicolans. . . . (Bishop 1999, 259)

Certainly I stretched the five-paragraph form with each long paragraph.
Still, that limitation and the additional demand of comparison-and-contrast
structure allowed me to discuss both locations—Alaska and Florida—in each
paragraph and to do so compactly and lyrically. Having constraints actually
freed me to make connections I might not otherwise have made had I wandered
in memory just waiting for patterns to appear. In this instance, by forcing
them, I found them. (Forcing can also have its downside, particularly if you are
of "the facts, just the facts, ma'am" school of nonfiction.)

5. *Ask, What did I put in, what did I leave out? What should I put in, what
should I leave out?*
It is hard to make ethical decisions until you consider the implications of your
choices. There are several schools of thought about who owns a story. Some
writers will never be comfortable sharing their interpretation of a shared experience so long as that parent or close friend is alive and could potentially read
the narrative. Like Bronwyn Williams, they ask: "Who is implicated in the
shaky memories I write about? Who is hurt by my lies? Whose story am I
allowed to tell? And why am I allowed to tell it, simply because I am a writer?"
(Williams 2003, 297). For others, like Mary Clearman Blew, the answer is fairly
obvious:

> Students often ask, what can you decently write about other people? Whose
> permission do you have to ask? What can you decently reveal about yourself?
>   I can only speak for myself. I own my past and my present. Only I can
> decide whether or how to write about it. (2002, 234)

Remember, no one sees your draft until you're ready to share it. At times
you'll find it useful to take a breath and tell your computer exactly what's going
on: type out the deepest truths you know—you get to save or delete that file—
and later, when you're ready, decide what, or even if, to share. Be aware, though,
that what you don't say in a draft can be as confusing to readers as what you do
say. For instance, by avoiding, with good reason, the reasons for a good friend's
alcoholism as well as deciding you're not ready to speculate about your parent's
relationship to the drug, your story about the stress you experienced during your
senior year may be drained of import because you are leaving a consequential
ellipsis that a reader senses more than sees, a hole in the text that he needs filled
in order to understand your aims. You think you're just talking about divorce,
friendship, and leaving home, but addictions might have unignorable impacts on
those relationships and events. How will you know? Explore in the safety of your

revisions and drafts; even if you decide this is an essay better written at another point in your life and even if you don't use these drafts, they'll help you clarify your stance toward the ownership and import of shared stories.

Try This

Explore what is almost but not quite said (a prompt suggested by Peter Elbow and Pat Belanoff in several of their accounts about ways to respond to writing). When readers tell you they are confused by certain parts of your piece, write more deeply into those sections of your draft (think of this as a hypertext link; maybe you'll actually make it one later). If you're comfortable in conversation, simply ask them to tell you what they think is being avoided and decide later what to do with that information. When you can, revise to include some aspect that you have ignored or avoided and then revise it out again in a subsequent draft (if necessary).

> There were a few things I left out about our visit and I couldn't figure a way to weave them into what I already had. Sister Fay [a fortune teller] told me a great deal about her life in Italy and her home, and I couldn't figure out why she was doing this. Maybe she wasn't getting the kind of reaction she wanted from me? I wasn't sure and didn't know how to put this here.
> —from Carlyn's process narrative on her essay "Paying Attention to Sister Fay"

> Something I feel I should mention here is that I eliminated one of the characters. I took Ryan out of the draft because I thought he detracted from the gravity of the piece. I think he took away from the impact of the opening. . . . Also, Ryan would not have been upset that I cut him from the scene. In the end, I don't think this decision degrades the ethical integrity of the piece; I think it improves it by more effectively communicating the main idea of the piece.
> —Jeff, on his essay "High Tide"

Sometimes you feel you shouldn't share certain elements of your lived life; sometimes you're not yet expert enough to do so effectively. Revising and publishing in safe locations—by sharing your work with friends, and eventually with editors and family—will help you discover what is best for your work.

6. *Ask, How does this story need to be told at this moment in my writing life?* If you turn prospector of your material, as suggested earlier, you're likely to hit rich veins of material that you will feel obliged to explore again and again. Personal essays have themes because authors' lives have themes. The pleasure of writing in this genre is that of working yet again to enact your vision, to tell your story, to understand events. Discussing the memoir, Jocelyn Bartkevicius reminds us of those return journeys to the same topic when she explains: "The pitted, nearly invisible landscape of the past is a mysterious, inviting place. Each

exploration reveals a different topography" (2002, 226). Sometimes you can speed up the process of return and reexcavation through revision.

Try This

Recast the same narrative in as many of the following formats as possible:

- Straight time—Move from past to present.
- Modified time—Play with flashback, flash-forward, prequel, sequel.
- Cinematic time—Film the narrative, shape it into scenes, and reorder the scenes.
- Photographic time—Provide a set of ten verbal photos; arrange them in order and/or shuffle the deck (see Fulwiler 1998; Root 2002).
- Collage time—Juxtapose elements by random arrangement or synchronous themes: organize in five sections using flower names, four sections using seasons, six sections, each named for a family member or a town; explore a metaphor; use color to write a section or an entire text, for example, blue-wash a paragraph with blue-related words, and so on.
- Imitate Akira Kurosawa's use of time in the movie *Rashoman*—replay the same incident from the point of view of each character involved; added up, let them narrate for the narrator.

> At its inception . . . this essay felt like a train wreck. I started out writing about my father, then about how my parents met, then all of a sudden I was writing about a close friend to whom I hadn't been quite honest about my feelings—*not* something I wanted to write about. I don't think I've ever done more drafts of a piece this short. . . . I've done at least two or three more, structural changes involving my recasting (and recasting and recasting) of the ending. . . . I'm definitely not going to send it out as non-fiction, though the writing seems too strong for it to simply go in a drawer. I might try to fictionalize it and send it out that way. I think it might be interesting to change the season to winter and play with heat and coldness . . . that walk home would be so much better in snow anyway. That's the fiction writer in me, I suppose, revising my life.
> —Maggie, process note to "Kamikazes"

Most writers, as Maggie does here, make decisions they didn't expect to have to make when their drafting takes them down unexpected corridors.

7. *Ask, What have I learned?*

> If I have told the story well and true, the story that I alone have lived to tell, readers will understand it in their own ways and will enrich their understanding of the world we share. (Bloom 2003, 288)

The experienced writer, like Lynn Bloom, has learned how to trust her faculties; she knows she'll generally make the right decision, she has a wealth of tools she can employ, she's ready to tell her story. For the novice writer, this sense of being sure of delivering a true and understandable text to a willing reader comes more slowly. The decisions writers make instruct them in future decisions. But they do so only if writers analyze what they have accomplished on a regular basis. The young writer (and the writer who wishes to increase his abilities) learns from reflecting on what he put in and what he left out. A good vehicle for this sort of examination is the writing process narrative.

Try This

Tell the story of your draft. How, where, when, why, and with what success and what frustrations did you compose it? Now, project your essay. If you had one week, what would you add? Two weeks? Six months? Five years? How would you revise this text if your circumstances were materially or dramatically changed: you're now married (and you weren't then); one person in the story is no longer alive; you're no longer poor; you've won the lottery; and so on.

> Had I more time, I think I would go back to Sister Fay and write several episodes about her and our time together. I would ask more questions about the cards and read more about Tarot so as to inform a little of their meaning in the piece. I would probably take written notes at her place, and I think I would be more willing to talk with Sister Fay more about my life.
> —Carlyn, in her process narrative about "Paying Attention to Sister Fay"

> If I had two more weeks to work on this project, I would try to revise the paragraph that begins, "the condition he described was unfathomable to me." I always feel like I have at least one weak paragraph in a piece, and this one happens to be it. I would also contact Ryan to see if he remembers things the way I do. I think it would be interesting to compare memories. I'd also like to ask him how he felt about me cutting him out of the piece.
> —Jeff, on his essay "High Tide"

Carlyn wishes for a more focused interview (but time was short that summer), and Jeff would like to spend time polishing his prose and consulting with a friend from the time he is describing. I've learned that writers often wish they were less lazy or less pushy with their drafts, that they had more time or had taken a different direction, that they could share the draft with the person discussed or spend more time collecting facts before the newspaper had to be published, and so on. Some of these desires can never be addressed, but you'll find that many of them can. It's up to you. The text is yours. If you started with an assignment, now is the time to take control and learn even more—for yourself, for your reader.

8. Ask, What have my readers learned?
To focus on your goals and aims for your text is important, but eventually, you'll want to share the results of your labor, to make last revisions with readers in mind.

Which means you need to create readers, ideal or real, and move toward them. It's not an easy task, but it's one you improve at over time. Patricia Hampl characterizes her reader as "a cat, endlessly fastidious, capable, by turns, of mordant indifference and riveted attention, luxurious, recumbent, and ever poised. Whereas the writer is absolutely a dog, panting and moping, too eager for an affectionate scratch behind the ears, lunging frantically after any old stick thrown in the distance" (Hampl 2002, 263). Her images capture the difficulty of matching hope to reality, of being a dog who can please a cat.

You should be aware that other readers worry about being told too much by writers, of being turned, unwillingly, into a voyeur of sorts. Bronwyn Williams registers his uneasiness:

> Yet for all the power that reading about real events holds for me, reading creative nonfiction often makes me cringe. It's not the revelations writers make about themselves that make me uncomfortable; it's what the writers reveal about others. I can't but wonder what must their children/parents/ spouses/friends think about being written of in this way? Even if the stories are true, it is their lives that are on display as much as the writers'. Such concerns gnaw at me even as I write this essay. (2003, 296)

Writers of creative nonfiction have to learn to determine when they have written just enough or far too much. For most of us, that means years of working in the genre and learning from our revisions.

Try This

Share with peers who are attempting similar writing challenges. Also, if possible, find someone concerned with the events you narrate to see how she reads your rendering. If you're writing about your parents during the Vietnam conflict, try to find a reader who also lived through that time period. If you're discussing coming of age in a new century, ask contemporaries who have had a similar experience to read at least one of your drafts. Overall, share your writing with others who are writing in the same genre: your classmates, members of an informal writing group, an email writing partner.

> In the first version, my overall point wasn't that clear. It seemed like just a collection of interesting family stories. It was clear to me, but didn't make it to the page. It just interests me the way stories about people help you understand their personalities. In the second version, "Connecting the Generations," I think the point was muddled by the fact that I jettisoned many of the stories and focused only on my great-grandfather, which made it seem like I was a little obsessed with him, personally. "Why him?" my peer reviewers asked.
> —Sandra, in her process memo for "All I'm Left With"

To understand readers, you need readers of all kinds and, if possible, throughout your drafting process. You need readers you can trust and you need to trust

Ten

If the Poet Wants to Be a Poet

Laura Newton

If the poet wants to be a poet, the poet must force the poet to revise.
If the poet doesn't wish to revise, let the poet abandon poetry and
take up stamp-collecting or real estate.

—Donald Hall

In many ways, revising poetry is radically different from revising other kinds
of writing. The canvas is much smaller, for one. In a poem, each word is a larger
percentage of the whole than a word in a short story or a novel, so the stakes
are higher; the placement of each word matters more; the relationship of each
word to the words around it matters, and the way words are grouped into lines
matters. Revising a poem can be easier than revising a piece of prose writing,
simply because a poem is usually short enough that the entire revision can take
place in an hour. Yet, revising a poem can be much more exasperating, because
a poet can tinker endlessly; there are almost infinite permutations of each poem.

Much of what we call revision is second nature to a working poet. Revision
begins with the first line committed to memory or to the page, maybe even the
first word. It begins the first time a poet crosses something out or deletes
something. It begins the minute the poet pauses during the act of writing and
writes the thought that emerged after the pause rather than the one that was
there before it. We all revise. We can't help ourselves. For many of us it's a
difficult and tortuous process, but it doesn't have to be. Not only can revision
be fun; it can be the most challenging and exciting stage of the life of the poem.

In *Creating Poetry*, John Drury lists the revising idiosyncrasies of six
famous poets.

Richard Hugo says to use a # 2 pencil and cross out vigorously rather than
erase corrections. Robert Graves used different writing implements for drafts
and revision. Donald Justice has experimented with different colored pens to
indicate different stages of revision. Robert Lowell made corrections with red
ink on typescript, even minutes before walking on stage to give a poetry
reading. Elizabeth Bishop left blanks in her drafts for words she couldn't get
right and taped the drafts above her desk. Shelley, in the flush of inspiration,

125

often left blanks for phrases or lines he didn't have time to mull over in the
surge of writing a first draft. (1991, 192)

While these behaviors are fascinating, they are more like poetry fetishes than
like revision strategies. They describe the rituals many poets create for tracking the changes in a poem but suggest little about how to go about changing
the poem itself.

Much is made of Allen Ginsberg's remark "first thought, best thought," and
we are reminded that Keats wrote complete drafts the first time around. But
these are exceptions, not the rule, and I'd guess that even Ginsberg and Keats
composed their first thoughts mentally and completed many revisions in their
heads before their poems made it to the page.

Few of us are us are as committed to revision as Donald Hall, who told
Martin Lammon in a 1993 interview that he has revised one poem as many as
six hundred times. Lammon remarked that Dylan Thomas "claimed to work
through a poem by writing two lines a day, finishing each line before moving
on toward the completed poem." Hall replied that he needs hundreds of nights
of sleeping on the poem before he can judge it. It is those hundreds of possible versions that make poetry so exciting and so frustrating at the same time.

Revision is a very different proposition for beginning writers than it is for
experienced writers. The students in my freshman introduction to poetry class
believe that a poem arrives full-blown from the forehead of Zeus. They believe
that it is the inspired word of their own small poetry god, and it cannot be tinkered with or it will lose its power. They also believe that a poem can mean
anything; some of them believe a poem *should* mean anything, and so they
resist all efforts to sharpen the way it says something, to make it more concrete,
more imagistic, more tangible, or more specific. They have not yet grasped the
awful power of language, the way it can start a revolution, provoke a nation
to genocide, start or end a relationship, sway people's hearts and minds. And
so in defense of their innocence, they resist any approach that will make them
examine the way they use language or the way other poets use language.

Experienced writers are more likely to acknowledge the value of revision.
We know that Yeats revised poems for years after he'd written them, even after
they'd been published. Donald Hall says that you should have one hundred reasons for each thing you do with a poem, for every comma, line break, and article. When I first read this, I thought he must be exaggerating to illustrate his
point, and perhaps he is. But the statement illustrates the great care with which
the poet should approach each poem. The point, he said, is to be as conscious
as you can be, knowing all along that you can't be completely conscious.

I suppose it's possible that all writers are obsessive revisers, and poets are
the extremists of the writing world. Of course, how you define revision comes
into play here, as well. I think we'd all agree that if you rework the line breaks,
that's revision. If you rephrase things to up the internal rhyme, that's revision.
If you cut whole sections or go through the poem and remove all the articles
you can do without, that's revision. How about this: If you change one word

and then reprint the poem to see how it looks on the page, have you revised the poem? Does that count as one of the six hundred times? I'd say it does. It might be useful to ask yourself where you draw the line. What is and isn't revision when you are working with a poem?

I tend to write first drafts that are what Richard Howard calls "loose baggy monsters." Poems rarely come to me with clear line breaks, phrasing, or images. Rather, poems come to me buried in large unmanageable narratives or jumbles of dreamlike ideas or in a stream of physical impressions. So the first step, the first draft, is often like going to the woods and using a chain saw to cut a large burl off a tree. Then I have to get it on the truck, wrestle it home, and set it up in the middle of the shop floor. That's the hard part, and everything else is a whittling away to find the nose, the ear, the breast, or the hip of the poem.

Having first written too much, I find great pleasure in chipping away what doesn't need to be there so that what does need to be there is revealed. However, new things often find their way into the poem as I revise. My husband is a bowl turner. (He's also an emergency room nurse. Both of his major tasks in life involve repairing or revising.) When a bowl is finished, particularly if it's a bowl made for art's sake, rather than for utility, it often has holes or pockets where the natural formation of the wood is spalted or has an interesting ding. Sometimes the bowl literally explodes during the turning and must be thrown out or reconstructed into something different from its original design. When this happens he sometimes mixes wood particles, sawdust, or even turquoise dust with glue and fills in the crack or the hole, making the bowl infinitely more interesting and lovely. Often the most exciting kind of revision is the kind where I am gluing word sawdust, mixed with new material I have unearthed, back into the poem. This new material is sometimes simply an extension of the original poem, but it is often information and ideas and images found in whatever I am reading or doing during the revision stage of the poem.

Hundreds of pages have been written about how to revise; much of it has been written about how to revise poetry. If you type the words "revision" or "revising" and "poetry" into any search engine on the Internet, you'll get fifty or sixty options, which would seem like enough hits to keep a writer busy all day. Yet many of the poetry texts I've surveyed, in print and online, simply extol the virtue of revision. While they exhort the poet to revise, they say little about *how* to revise.

I'd like to suggest two overarching revision strategies here. The first strategy is to examine how you revise and to learn from your own process. The second is to examine, and then have fun with, what provokes you to revise.

Examine How You Revise and Learn from Your Own Process

This examination approach is designed to help you determine what your current revision behavior is and to figure out if it is useful or if it is driving you crazy. Some revision strategies are very useful; others are little more than avoidance behaviors, wheel spinners, ways to pretend you're working when you're really afraid to do the difficult work of really changing the poem you're working on or of starting a new poem. The simple description of this approach is *Observe your own revision strategy*. Codify it. Woodworking is my metaphor for revision, and it helps me see it as a stage of the art itself, to be more relaxed and excited by the process. I imagine that you have your own metaphor (or several) for revision. It might be useful to articulate it, to write it down and polish it up. Use it according to the code for a while. Revise that code. You can begin by trying to determine what your own revision strategy is, to elevate it to a conscious set of steps, at least for a while. Then, once you are aware of it and have tweaked it into a useful set of steps, you can let it sink under the surface once again until the next time you need to adjust it.

If you draft on a computer, the easiest way to do this is to use a combination of the "save as" function and the editing function of your word-processing software. As you are revising, track the changes with the software's tracking function. Let it cross out old text and underline and highlight new text in red so that you'll be able to see in a glance what you changed between one draft and the next. Next, set up a folder for each poem you are working on. Each time you finish a draft, do two things. Save the changes using the "save as" function rather than the "save" function. Then add a number to the name of each successive draft and drop it into the right folder. So if you are working on a poem called "Breath," you'll have Breath 1, Breath 2, Breath 3, and so on. If you draft by hand, you'll need a manila folder for each poem and a paper copy of each draft. The second thing to do is to note how each revision came about, what provoked it. Did you revise in response to feedback, in response to the poem itself, or just to see what the poem would do if you poked it?

This phase of your exploration shouldn't be hurried. Just do it for a while. I'd suggest that you do this with at least five to ten poems before you begin to analyze your own process. Then spread the drafts out on a large table and begin to map and discover what it is that you are doing and why.

Examine and Have Fun with What Provokes You to Revise

We are usually provoked to revise by one of two things. One of these provocations comes from a reader in a workshop or in a less formal setting. The other comes from the poem itself. There is a third reason to revise, however. We can revise for the fun of it, to see where else the poem might go or what it might turn into in a new form or with a new approach. Let's look at each of these approaches to revising to see what we can do to maximize the value of each kind of revision.

or create more space inside it. Sometimes we need to be pried loose from an old rut. Sometimes we need to play with words. This is the kind of revising that I find to be the most interesting.

Tom Hunley, a member of my poetry group, loves to tinker with nonce forms. He gives us assignments in new forms, hybrid forms, or made-up forms. The assignments, based on hybrids such as a haiku sonnet or, my favorite, a pantoum sonnet, are great fun and excellent revision strategies. The haiku sonnet is a series of four haiku followed by a couplet. Pantoum sonnets mimic the Shakespearean sonnet in that they have fourteen lines, three quatrains, and a couplet, but the quatrains use the pantoum repeating pattern, while the couplet performs its traditional role of generalizing or wrapping up. It's up to you, or your group, or the poem, to decide which of the other rules of the blended forms the poem must follow. Lewis Turco's *Book of Forms* (2002) is an invaluable tool for learning about forms and finding ideas for mixing and matching various aspects of form. Remember: All forms were invented by someone.

Another member of my group, David Higginbotham, uses translation software to find interesting variations on the language he is using. He plugs the poem into a translation website, then translates it into another language, such as Spanish, then into a third language, such as Italian. The final step is to translate the poem back into English. This won't work if you translate the poem from one language to another and right back again. You'll just end up with what you started with. Something about the third language is like a game of gossip. The language changes in fascinating ways, often revealing cultural assumptions or phrasing that we've never really understood. In David's example, the "quest for the abominable snowman" became "the questioning marionette of the repulsive snow." While you might not use the new language you discover through this process, it could illuminate the meaning or deepen your understanding of the language you are using.

Paisley Rekdal says that each of her poems tells at least two or three stories. If the poem is too obvious or too still, research a concept or image in the poem, then layer what you've learned into the poem, even if, or especially if, the direction it takes confuses you or pulls you underwater or underground. If the poem reminds you of another, seemingly unrelated story or image, you might write that thread into the poem. For instance, a poem I have been working on recently is called "Breathing." It begins with an exploration of a quotation from a scientist about how we breathe in actual molecules of items in the world around us. It then folds in a reference to my grandfather's saying that every child has to eat a peck of dirt before he's grown. Wendy Bishop, who shared with me the quotation that started me thinking about the poem, suggested that the poem could explore pica, the mineral deficiency that makes some women eat dirt, and so it weaves a meditation on breathing in molecules with a memory of my grandfather with an image of a pregnant woman eating dirt.

Learn the Tools of the Trade

Of course, the most essential revision strategy is to cultivate and nurture our interest in language and in the many uses of language. Mary Oliver says that the revision process requires energy, honesty, and patience, "but nothing is so helpful as an interest in language that amounts almost to a mania" (1998, 96). Much of revising poetry is craft. We can make a serviceable piece of furniture with very basic and simple tools: a single saw, a hammer, and some nails. But we can make a gorgeous piece of furniture using the more specific tools of a woodworker: a planer, a joiner, a lathe, a scroll saw. For a poet, the simple tools are the words, figures of speech, and line breaks. The more specific tools are enjambment, caesura, assonance and consonance, the many varieties of rhyme and rhythm and the structures of the couplet, the quatrain, the sonnet, and the villanelle. To use these tools, even as faint echoes in our work, we must know what they are, and we must read the works of poets who use them and use them well.

I once heard the poet David Kirby describe the reference books that are always on the shelf right next to his desk. When I got home, I checked my own shelf, where I found a dictionary, a synonym finder, a rhyming dictionary, the *Ultimate Visual Dictionary*, Petersons' field guide to eastern birds, Kirby's *Dictionary of Contemporary Thought*, John Drury's *Poetry Dictionary* and *Creating Poetry*, Wendy Bishop's *Thirteen Ways of Looking for a Poem*, Mary Oliver's *Rules for the Dance*, and Mary Kinzie's *Poet's Guide to Poetry*. I also found there *The Rose*, by Li-Young Lee, *One Above and One Below*, by Erin Belieu, several volumes of *Best American Poetry*, and Shakespeare's *Sonnets*. Because I am interested in the intersection between science and religion, I have a collection of books like Capra's *Tao of Physics* and *A Brief History of Time*, by Steven Hawking. When the poetry cools down or needs a shove, I read these books and let them settle into my psyche.

Amy Lowell said, "All poetry consists of flashes of the subconscious mind and Herculean efforts on the part of the conscious mind to equal them. That is where training comes in. The more expert the poet, the better will he fill in the gaps in his inspiration. Revising is the act of consciously improving what was unconsciously done" (quoted in Oliver 1998, 95). Through revision we can train ourselves to be better poets, to elevate the steps and the tools of our craft to a conscious level and at the same time have fun doing it.

Works Cited

Drury, John. 1991. *Creating Poetry*. Cincinnati: Writer's Digest.

Hall, Donald. 1994. "Flying Revision's Flag." An interview with Martin Lammon, originally published in *Kestral*, 1993, from *Death to the Death of Poetry*, by Donald Hall, University of Michigan Press, 1994. The Academy of American poets website: <www.poets.org/poems/prose.cfm>.

Oliver, Mary. 1998. *The Rules for the Dance*. Boston: Houghton Mifflin.

Works Referenced

Bishop, Wendy. 2000. *Thirteen Ways of Looking for a Poem*. New York: Longman.

Belieu, Erin. 2000. *One Above and One Below*. Port Townsend, WA: Copper Canyon.

Capra, Fritjof. 2000. *The Tao of Physics: An Exploration of the Parallels Between Modern Physics and Eastern Mysticism*. 4th ed. Boston: Shambhala.

Drury, John. 1995. *The Poetry Dictionary*. Cincinnati: Story.

Evans, Jo, ed. 1994. *Ultimate Visual Dictionary*. New York: Dorling Kindersley.

Hawking, Stephen. 1988. *A Brief History of Time*. New York: Bantam.

Kinzie, Mary. 1999. *A Poet's Guide to Poetry*. Chicago: University of Chicago Press.

Kirby, David. 1984. *Dictionary of Contemporary Thought*. London: MacMillan.

Lee, Li-Young. 1986. *The Rose*. Brockport, NY: BOA Editions.

Peterson, Roger Tory. 1980. *Eastern Birds*. Boston: Houghton Mifflin.

Turco, Lewis. 2000. *The Book of Forms: A Handbook of Poetics*. 3d ed. Lebanon, NH: University Press of New England.

Eleven

The Making of a Poem, Live and Uncensored

Dana Kantrowitz

Sometimes I get jealous of singers. Not because I'm tone-deaf in both ears, but because a singer's words disappear into the air as easily as the air filled her lungs. And no one will know if a singer stopped before the song was over, or if she hit the wrong note, or forgot the words. Unless, of course, she's singing in front of a live audience. But the act of singing itself is forgiving because it forgets the singer's past—unlike writing. Writing is an old friend with a grudge. It remembers your old journals, your composition essays, and your first poem. But like an old friend, it has grown on you, and you have grown with it. For that reason, and many others, writers are interested in the process of writing, how we move from those journals to an acknowledgeable draft, a polished collection, a Pulitzer Prize. We talk about it every day in our rhetoric and style classes, at public readings, in creative writing workshops, in analytical essays, in interviews, and in private conversations over wine and cigarettes. We are asking each other *How do you do it? What works for you? When do you know a work is finished? Where does your style come from?*

Admittedly, I know nothing of earning Pulitzer Prizes or even publishing polished collections. I'm a graduate student in search of a kindhearted poetry editor and an affordable, yet stylish, sofa. But my anonymity has its advantages. Without the fear of exposing and demystifying something sacred like the disappointing lyrics of an imperceptible classic rock song you've been humming since you were fourteen, I can share something that resembles what every writer does in private, in a tiny room with an open window, a candle burning, or a sleeping dog at her feet. I'm going to write a poem from scratch.

Another wide-eyed young writer by the name of Leslie Whatley recently told me he's interested in exploring the idealized vision he has of himself as a writer. I'm examining not the vision, but the reality of it, the messy reality of putting words on a page. In the process, I hope to uncover some things:

- how changing a single word, image, line, or line break alters the focus, style, voice, message, and/or tone of my poem as it's being written

- how the idea or knowledge of an audience affects my poem as I'm writing it

- how the process of writing helps me discover what I'm trying to say, what the poem wants to say
- how metaphors happen, when they are working, and when they are not
- how beginnings and endings happen
- how my surroundings, mood, and current life situations affect the poem
- how I get mentally and physically prepared to write and what I do after writing
- how and when I get into the flow or the zone and how and when I get stuck and deal with writer's block

If a curious new writing student or a seasoned writing instructor wanted to try something like this, to examine her personal writing experiences in a new way, she would most likely consider an entirely different set of objectives. But the process of establishing goals before the actual writing begins truly helps to give focus and purpose to this kind of exercise. The idea is to use yourself as a guinea pig and act as both the lab rat (another fine rodent metaphor) and the twisted scientist. In order to collect useful data, I tape-recorded myself while I was writing a new poem and verbalized, in the only way I knew how, the many thoughts that tackled my brain, hoping that what would be captured on tape wouldn't resemble the sound of a churning garbage disposal. I took the idea of using a tape recorder from a similar, yet much more lengthy and clinical, case study of professional writer Donald M. Murray,[1] conducted by Carol Berkenkotter. Berkenkotter recognized the "need to replicate naturalistic studies of skilled and unskilled writers before we can begin to infer patterns that will allow us to understand the writing process in all of its complexity" (1983, 167). And Murray himself claimed he had "long felt the academic world [was] too closed. . . . Writers should, instead of public readings, give public workshops in which they write in public, allowing the search for meaning to be seen" (1983, 169). This search for meaning is where my writing process begins.

For the purpose of this study, I sat down about a week ago (I'll talk about procrastination in a moment) with a tape recorder and rambled about the general feeling and the meaning I was hoping to discover and convey with this new poem. Normally, I don't sit down with a tape recorder or even a pen and paper or notes of any kind when I plan on writing a poem. I'm guessing that my writing process is different from most writers', as I hear a lot about prewriting, journal keeping, character sketches, and notes scribbled on napkins in coffeehouses across America. But, over time, a writer learns what works for her and what

---

1. Donald M. Murray was a professor of English at the University of New Hampshire at the time of the study. He agreed to work with Carol Berkenkotter, who later published her findings, paired by the journal editors with a response essay by Murray. See Carol Berkenkotter, 1983, "Decisions and Revisions: The Planning Strategies of a Publishing Writer" (*College Composition and Communication* 34 (2): 156–69); Donald Murray, 1983, "Response of a Laboratory Rat—or, Being Protocoled" (*College Composition and Communication* 34 (2): 169–72).

feels more like eating French fries with a spoon because someone told her it was the right way to do it. What doesn't work for me, and what I quickly realized was making me hate my vague idea of this new poem, is speaking to a tape recorder about my vague idea of this new poem. A half hour of talking in a room with a desk and seven Beatles posters was just enough time to convince myself that the idea of a poem about my boyfriend hunting and my mixed feelings toward this hobby of his was underdeveloped, too simplistic, and on the whole, not worthy of being the one poem that I would case-study.

Then I made an executive decision to extend my deadline, so here is where procrastination appears. For the next week, I went on long walks around a lovely manmade lake, baked a yellow cake, and got to know my dogs a little better. But the poem was waiting for me, lurking behind trees, burning my cake, and convincing my dogs that I'm not worth their time. And yesterday I sat down for the first time in a week to write a poem about hunting. I didn't waste any time with prewriting or prethinking. I just turned on my laptop and my recorer and said, aloud, "I'm going to write a poem now."

This is what came out over the course of about fifteen minutes:

At the North Florida Fair
in the pavilion with the floor of dirt and hay
I touched a yak.
Its face:
a nose the size of a shoe box,
its tongue, a black leather shoe,
softened from years of grazing the body's rugged landscape.
But

Listening to the tape, I was surprised by the sighs of frustration, the number of questions I asked myself, and the long moments of silence when the thoughts were moving too quickly to catch and spit out of my mouth. I could hear the sound of overwhelming uncertainty, and at the end of this snippet of a stanza, I said, "I don't know what I mean." I settled for words or phrases that I didn't really trust, but I was willing to keep them on the page in order to move on. Seeing words up and about, rather than keeping all possibilities in their chairs until the perfect one quietly raised its hand, kept the poem alive in this critical state.

Every time I hesitated, started to lose the feeling (I *felt* something almost immediately), or forgot where I was going with this image of a yak, I read the words from start to finish, start to finish, until a new phrase or word made its way to the page. Each time I read the entire snippet, I picked up something I had missed before. I changed what was originally a comma after "face" to a colon in order to open up the description of the animal's face like a scene in itself. I tapered the wording, trimming the line "its tongue, the size of a black leather shoe" to "its tongue, a black leather shoe." And I morphed the phrase "flattened from years of moving across the body's _____ landscape" to "softened from years of grazing the body's rugged landscape." I wanted the *texture* of the tongue, rather than just the shape of it, since the lines were already full of visual images. I searched for the active verb, the verb the reader could see, and chose *grazing* (which also denotes the action of an animal) over *moving across*. I left a blank before "landscape," knowing that I wanted an adjective there, but nothing came to mind until the rest of the words were already in place.

So many considerations went into these seven lines, but I still had only a general sense of where this was going. The idea of the fair was based on my experience the weekend before. During my week of lovely procrastination, I went to the fair and, of course, visited the petting zoo. Productive procrastination. Somehow my mind made a connection between my feelings of touching that massive and foreign animal and my boyfriend's hunting trip earlier that week. There was something there, but I wasn't exactly sure what it was. Yet, I was confident that writing the poem would help me figure it out. I'm truly an impatient writer (and reader), but I've learned to know when an extra hour or four at the desk is worth it. Maybe if I were more of a beginning writer, I would have turned off my laptop without saving—taken another walk around the lake. But I know that I can make almost anything work if *I'm* willing to work, that I can always delete the words that make me hate what I'm writing, that I am actually in control of this wild beast of a thing.

So I played with it for a while and soon felt the need to extend the image of the yak to include its situation (living in captivity) and my feelings about a wild and majestic animal being kept in such an environment. But, the poet in me knows that being blunt and whiny is not the most effective and artistic way to convey my feelings. I turned to image, once again, to carry the emotion of the poem. The additional metaphor and simile came forth with little effort in a pleasingly short amount of time:

> At the North Florida Fair
> in the pavilion with the floor of dirt and hay,
> I touched the face of a yak:
> its nose, the size of a shoe box,
> its tongue, a black leather shoe,
> softened from years of grazing the body's rugged landscape.
> The body:
> a range of small-scaled mountains
> like those in the town of a model train set,
> a fixture surrounded by a fence.

The arrival of the second stanza was a serious attempt to bring tension to the poem by introducing my boyfriend, the hunter.

> At the North Florida Fair
> in the pavilion with the floor of dirt and hay,
> I touched the face of a yak:

its nose, the size of a shoe box,
its tongue, a black leather shoe,
softened from years of grazing the body's rugged landscape.
The body:
a range of small-scaled mountains
like those in the town of a model train set,
a fixture surrounded by a fence.

The man I love
spent the early morning hours eight feet above the forest floor,
suspended in time.
His back supported by the bark of an old pine,
his feet clutched to the metal bar of a tree-stand,
his bowstring, taut against the autumn wind,
his eyes, wide and brown as a deer's.

Uncomfortable with the sound and connotation of the word *boyfriend*, I opted for "the man I love." Part of my mistrust of certain words and phrases is their connotations and the possibility that using them will make my poem sound silly, lighthearted (when it's not intended to be), or immature. With this stanza, the amount of options was overwhelming at one point. I couldn't decide at what images to point my camera or in what order to arrange the pictures. But the language itself just flowed through me in about fifteen minutes. What I had hoped to understand by listening to the tape, what I wanted to hear in the back of my own throat, was the birth of poetic language, the pip of the egg of a metaphor. But it wasn't there. By this time, I was in the sought-after zone and practically forgot that I was talking into a tape recorder. Like Donald Murray, "I [do] not assume . . . that what I said reflected all that was taking place. It did reflect what I was conscious of doing, and a bit more. My articulation was an accurate reflection of the kind of talking I do to myself. . . ." At many times the only articulation I could produce was silence.

I took a moment to notice the line lengths. I broke the lines in this new stanza in ways that generally mirrored those in the previous stanza for the sake of consistency and because I didn't want any one particular line to stand out as too long, to draw attention to itself. Then I was ready to move on, but not until I introduced the first stanza to the second stanza. It was as if they didn't know each other but were about to meet at the altar. The first stanza needed a reference to time of day so the transition to the second stanza and the shift in time would be clear.

High above the dusty plot of a country fair just south of Georgia,
clouds white as sheets on a clothesline, hung motionless in the afternoon sun.
Under the pavilion with the floor of dirt and hay,
I touched the face of a yak:
its nose, the size of a shoe box,
its tongue, a black leather shoe,
softened from years of grazing the body's rugged landscape.

The body:
a range of small-scaled mountains
like those in the town of a model train set,
a fixture surrounded by a fence.

The man I love
spent the early morning hours eight feet above the forest floor,
suspended in time.
His back supported by the bark of an old pine,
his feet clutched to the metal bar of a tree-stand,
his bowstring, taut against the autumn wind,
his eyes, wide and brown as a deer's.

Immediately, I didn't like the presence of clouds in my poem. Clouds seemed trite, like every worthwhile description had been tagged before I even stepped onto the playing field. And I felt that I was giving too much attention to the sky when all I wanted to do was create a sense of daylight. No matter how much I insisted that they weren't welcome, the clouds wouldn't budge.

Listening to the tape of myself mumbling the F-word in an empty room, I thought of Berkenkotter's statement: "writers *do* monitor and introspect about their writing simultaneously." Of course, I have known that about my own writing for years now, but I feel it is being ignored to some extent by writing instructors. Maybe you disagree or have no idea what I'm talking about, but my creative writing education harped on the word *revision*, yet maintained it as *an abstract concept, this otherworldly reseeing*, and a task separate from the process of "writing." I was told by writing instructors that writers plan, freewrite, create a single draft, put it aside, then revise until second, third, and final drafts appear. Why is a more organic and sloppy process, one that blends writing and revising into a beautiful hodgepodge, one that can be refined and mastered over time, considered of lesser value? Reflecting on his own methods of "teaching" the writing process (can it be taught at all?), Murray admitted he "find[s] it very difficult to make [his] students aware of the layers of concern through which the writing writer must oscillate at such a speed that it appears the concerns are dealt with instantaneously. Too often in [his] teaching and [his] publishing [Murray has] given the false impression that we do one thing, then another, when in fact we do many things simultaneously. And the interaction between these things is what we call writing" (172).

As a student of writing, I've kept my seemingly undesirable writing process a secret for years (while trying to master it at the same time), forging fictitious drafts for my writing instructors and wondering if there were others . . . like me. The act of tape-recording and scrutinizing your own writing and speaking voice is guaranteed to show you something in a way that's not unlike poking yourself with a stick.

Like the poems of my past, I continued writing this one by reading and rereading it from start to finish until another word, then another stanza, began to take shape.

High above the dusty plot of a country fair just south of Georgia,
clouds white as sheets on a clothesline
hung motionless in the afternoon sun.
Under a pavilion with a floor of dirt and hay,
I touched the face of a yak:
its nose, the size of a shoe box,
its tongue, a black leather shoe,
softened from years of grazing the body's rugged landscape.
The body:
a range of small-scaled mountains
like those in the town of a model train set,
a fixture surrounded by a fence.

Earlier that day, suspended in time
and the cool gray of dawn,
the man I love
held his breath eight feet above a forest floor.
His back supported by the bark of an old pine,
his feet clutched to the metal bar of a tree-stand,
his bowstring, taut against the autumn wind,
his eyes, wide and brown as a deer's.

With a quarter, he bought a handful of carrots,
for me to _____
but I pulled away from the yak's wide teeth
as they rubbed against my open palm.

Although it might be exhausting to see this fragment of a poem again and again, watching as it drags its feet like a child past her bedtime, I didn't sound tired of the poem when I was writing it. And I was surprised to find that I had been working on it for only an hour at this point. In my experience, the writing process is not like a marathon, but more like a game of chess in Central Park, the kind with a timer and two old men. Only I'm both of these guys—the writer and the editor.

But I'm not tempted to suggest that my approach, my lack of preparation, my process, or my poems are the preferred ones. In her article, Berkenkotter didn't have to tell me twice that "research on single subjects is new in our discipline; we need to bear in mind that each writer has his or her own idiosyncrasies" (167). And mine are clear: I left the room on three separate occasions just to be able to return to it with a fresh perspective—and a sliver of chocolate cake. Writers are notorious drinkers and smokers, but I prefer eating chocolate and watching mindless television for those much-needed mental hiatuses. It's no surprise that stepping away from your writing, whether it's to defrost the chicken, watch the mail being delivered across the street, or fold laundry, has the magical powers of rejuvenation. After fleshing out the third stanza, I felt comfortable leaving the room.

Having taken an unexpected four-hour break during which I didn't look at or really think about the poem, I realized that it wasn't a yak but a buffalo that I was seeing. The buffalo also served as a reminder of the hunt, an animal with a dominating presence but a prize for many hunters. I was working to make connections, both emotional and visual, between the scene at the fair and the scene in the forest.

High above the dusty plot of a country fair just south of Georgia,
clouds white as sheets on a clothesline
hung motionless in the afternoon sun.
Under a pavilion with a floor of dirt and hay,
I touched the face of a buffalo:
its nose, the size of a shoe box,
its tongue, a black leather shoe,
softened from years of grazing the body's rugged landscape.
The body:
a range of small-scaled mountains
like those in the town of a model train set,
a fixture surrounded by a fence.

Earlier that day, suspended in time
and the cool gray of dawn,
the man I love
held his breath eight feet above a forest floor.
His back supported by the bark of an old pine,
his boot heel clutched to the metal footrest of a tree-stand,
his bowstring, taught against the autumn wind,
his eyes, wide and brown as a deer's.

With a quarter, he bought me a handful of carrot-wedges
from a bearded man in overalls.
My thin forearm fit easily between the bars of the fence,
but I scraped my elbow pulling away from the buffalo's wide teeth
as they rubbed like a block of wet wood against my open palm.

The deepest woods have never heard the man I love laugh or cry,
or seen his head bowing over an open book or the bathroom sink.
But they know the man I never will:
swaying with a tree like a flake of its own bark,
smelling of decomposing leaves and the swampy bank of a nearby lake,
reading the length and color of shadows like lines on a map,
his heart pumping the very blood of the hunt.

Until I returned to reread what I had written, I hadn't really noticed that the poem was in past tense. Usually my poems are framed in present tense to create a sense of immediacy, and I like the sound of verbs without the -ed weighing them down. But in this case I suddenly realized that I had been writing in the past tense and attributed this to the intentional sense of reflection in the poem, as if the narrator is reflecting on her experiences rather than discovering something along with the reader. It's scary to admit that I often don't notice what I'm doing while I'm doing it. The line breaks happened almost without thought. And the words themselves—the shoe box and the shoe, the model train set, the autumn wind, the lines on a map—seemed to have come from somewhere beyond me, falling to my body like leaves from a tree.

The addition of the final stanza sucked me dry, but I was satisfied enough to put down the poem for the day. The structure was there, the images were working for me, and the overall tone and message were nearing the target. What I began at 11:00 A.M. I put to sleep at 7:45 that night.

The next evening I returned to it, not as happy with the simplicity of the emotion of the poem or the weak transitions and feeling that the opening was far too long. After a couple hours, a couple chocolate breaks, and a tremendous bout of indecision, the following four stanzas became what could be considered the official first draft, although I don't really consider this a draft. It's not so sloppy at this stage and I don't foresee it taking on tremendous changes in terms of form or content. I found the title hours later, after having reread the poem a handful of times.

The Hour Between Night and Day

Under a pavilion at a country fair just south of Georgia,
kneeling to a floor of dirt and hay,
I touched the face of a buffalo:
her nose, the size of a shoe box,
her tongue, a black leather shoe
softened from years of grazing the body's rugged landscape.
The body:
a range of small-scaled mountains
like those in the town of a model train set,
a fixture surrounded by a fence.

Earlier that day, suspended in time
and the cool gray of dawn,
the man I love held his breath
nineteen feet above a forest floor.
His back supported by the spine of an old pine,
his boot heel clutched to the metal footrest of a tree-stand,
his bowstring, taut against the autumn wind,
his eyes, wide and brown as a buck's.

With the change from our funnel cake and lemonades,
he bought me a handful of carrot-wedges
from a bearded man in overalls.
My thin forearm fit easily between the bars of the fence
and out to the buffalo who I imagined
had followed her brothers and sisters from a dusty plot in Montana
into an eighteen-wheeler.
But I scraped my elbow pulling away from her wide teeth
as they rubbed like a block of wet wood against my open palm.

The deepest woods have never heard the man I love laugh or cry,

or seen his head bowing over an open book or the bathroom sink.
But they know the man I never will:
swaying with a tree like a flake of its own bark,
smelling of decomposing leaves and the swampy bank of a nearby lake,
reading the length and color of shadows like lines on a map,
waiting for the rustle and crack of briars and palmettos, of muscles and bones,
surviving on the air and blood of the morning hunt.

I'm satisfied that this poem does most of what I want my poems to do: it uses concrete images, colors, numbers, textures, and sounds. The structure has a digestible form covered and smothered in my favorite fixings: lists, long and short lines and sentences, and a visual and audible sense of symmetry and balance. The language itself plays with the neighborhood kids: metaphor and simile. I think the voice is lacking. It's a bit bland and indistinguishable from most voices. And I still believe that the complexity of the emotion I was feeling toward my experience with animals versus that of my boyfriend might not be in there just yet. But, it's a poem that wasn't here two days ago, and one that you and I have never seen before.

As a relatively new writer, a student writer, and an aspiring writer, my writing life is moving faster than my own. Every so often it should be slowed down and studied like the mad science it truly is. Like Murray's experience, "this project reaffirmed what I had known, that there are many simultaneous levels of concern that bear on every line" (172). Taking the time to recognize, and even tape-record, the action of these levels at work can be a useful tool for writers of all levels in understanding and appreciating the writing process in all of its beauty and ugliness.

Twelve

Why Not Hypertext? Converting the Old, Interpreting the New, Revising the Rest

Jay Szczepanski

This essay assumes one of two things: you are writing with publishing to the Internet specifically fixed in your mind, or you're working on your second hypertext draft. On the other hand, this essay assumes one of two other things if the first two don't apply to you: you have written something on paper and you want to convert it to hypertext format, or you've plainly pasted your scribblings up on the Net and no one is reading them because they're (choose all that apply) boring/listless, unnavigable/unreadable.[1]

So, What Is Hypertext?

When we talk about hypertext, what is it, exactly, that we're talking about? Anything that fits on the Web? HTML-encoded documents? Emails? Synchronous communication (instant messaging)? In one way or another, I like to think that all of these (among others) have some elements of hypertext. When you write hypertext, you are conscious of how it *differs* from "regular writing," or paper-based composition—and being conscious of the writing behaviors that you develop and tap into is what will make a difference when you actually go to revise and edit the piece of hypertextual writing that you have produced.

When I say *differs*, I mean that you make conscious decisions about what to include or not include. Let's take an instant message (IM) conversation, for example. You log on and talk to your friend from high school. You know and understand that shorthand expressions (gtg, lol) and emoticons (☺ ☹) are acceptable ways for you to communicate together. Your reader and friend understands what it is that you're trying to say with very little effort. In essence,

---

1. I'll have to make a small disclaimer here before we get started. Hypertext is a developing and broad field, so much so that I've tried to shy away from those things that I think will either not be relevant or those things that change too quickly. For instance, I don't talk about *how* you should create a webpage. Mechanically, there are several ways to make one (HTML code, what-you-see-is-what-you-get editing programs that function a lot like word processors, templates . . .).

she has internalized the decoding mechanisms that make a conversation that consists of abbreviated language readable.

Honestly, I come to hypertext as a sort of lone ranger (lone stranger?). Sure, I knew and know how to work and prod a word-processing program, and I can browse the Internet. But, it never occurred to me that one day I would write anything *serious* that would make its way to the Web. Eventually, though, I was offered the opportunity to teach a class in digital discourse. It was a class that I had never taught before, the result of an overcrowded incoming freshman class.

How Do You Read It?

Whenever I introduce the concept of hypertext to my students, they look at me strangely and nod their heads to signify to me that they understand what I'm saying. Few of them ever really do know what I mean when I say *hypertext*, so I'm going to give you the same lecture that I give them. And bear in mind that this is only my interpretation of how hypertext can work. If you have one that works better for you, then I say go for it.

The Newspaper Theory

When I was younger, everyone said that the Internet would be the end of newspapers. People would, of course, get their news online. Many people in fact do this, but far more people don't. For some, it's the feel of paper in hand, and for others, it's an economic or class problem—they simply don't have access to the technology that can bring media like digital journalism to them, yet, newspapers have not died out. I doubt that they ever will, because I think that hypertext owes its readability to newspapers. Think about is this way: you buy or swipe a paper from somewhere. You bring it home, you sit down, and there you are. You're reading a newspaper. Except that this newspaper is about eighteen inches tall and a foot wide (unfurled). You might begin reading the headline. You might immediately turn to sports, the weather, or entertainment. You might read the whole page, or maybe just the cover story. Few, if any of us, read every article in the paper, top to bottom, front to back, in order, beginning to end. In fact, if you were to read the *New York Times* Sunday Edition from front to back, it would take you more than a week of uninterrupted reading in order to get through it all.

As a reader, it's all about being selective, and being *able* to be selective. Hypertext is like a newspaper. Often, you have a choice of what to read and what to leave behind. Certain hyperlinks will take you to one section of the paper, and other links take you to another. The main index is like the front page of the newspaper: it gives you a rundown of what's going on and where you can find it. Some individuals whom I know read only the business section and throw the rest away. As a writer, however, it's all about providing yourself and

your readers with direction and ease of navigation. And making your hypertext interesting.

Elements of Hypertext

Hypertext can be:
fluid
dynamic
confusing
chronological
spatial
atemporal
rigidly structured
incomplete
thematic
disheveled

Since hypertext can be all of these things and more, and since as a genre
of writing it's still a developing form of writing, I'm going to mention or deal
with only two types of hypertextual writing. The first is one that reminds me
of the role-playing game the Sims. In it, you assume an identity, and the
choices that you make within the game affect your interactions with your
neighbors, your health, your romantic relationships, your workplace life, and
your overall well-being. Working in hypertext is like role-playing in a sense:
the choices that *you* make so that your *reader* can make them are pivotal and
have far-reaching consequences. How the reader is able to navigate your maze
of writing speaks both to his choices and yours.

The other type of hypertext writing is for those of us who want to present our writing converted from bright white bond paper into something more
digital and worldly—maybe to share with parents, or maybe because your
teacher insists that you present her with an alternate format. Or, maybe you
really do have something to say (as I suspect you all do), and setting up a website to communicate to the masses best serves your purposes—and it's a
damned good excuse to dust off that manifesto or diatribe and get some more
mileage out of it.

Overall, however, I think that hypertext essays are perhaps the most fun
to read. You offer the reader definite choices, and you both get to play. Good
play equals good writing.

Revision Opportunities

Say that your instructor tells you that for your next paper you have to write for
the Web. Fair enough. Traditionally, I've found that my students attempt this
exercise by writing a paper as they normally would—either by longhand or in
a word-processing program. What I stress to them, however, is that when they
move to put this paper on the Internet, a whole new world of revision options

awaits them. I give them this list of items to consider when they work over their second drafts:

1. How will you convert the paper into a navigable hypertext document?
2. How will you arrange and rearrange text to make the reading experience more fluid?
3. What will you do with citations and the bibliography?
4. Will you add a table of contents or navigation menu? Should you?
5. Why not, if you're feeling ambitious, add hyperlinks—those usually blue underlined bits o' text?
6. What about pictures and photographs and other media? Are their additions appropriate? And what about copyright?
7. What about ancillary material?

It's impractical for me to show you what my students have done to their papers in order to hypertextualize them (their being on the Internet and all, not to mention the oftentimes temporary and fleeting experience of hypertext in general), but I'll describe as best I can the choices that a few of them have made. I'll go through the list one by one, since I think each item is important for hypertext revision.

Translating into Hypertext

How will you convert the paper into a navigable hypertext document? What are you going to do to your paper in order to make it readable on the Web?

Largely, it's the interpretation that's the most fun when you think about how you're going to rearrange your paper. It makes you think more consciously about what you write and where you put what you write. I think that that's the aim of writing anyway. We need to learn about the decisions that we make and why we make them. Hypertext takes us out of our comfort zone and puts us in a place where knowledge of the whys and hows are imperative.

I'll talk later about navigation menus, so I think that this space would be best served if we talk about what you can do to the body of the document. Linear writing is fine (and, largely, linear writing is what we prize in America), and maybe I'm a rebel, but I've never liked being *too* linear. Hypertext is your chance to mix it up, if you want. (Later on, you'll read about one of my student's experiments with nonlinear writing.)

Now, I know what you might say: my paper has no need for rearrangement. Perhaps, but how do you know? I'm not trying to second-guess you, but we're humans, and we don't like change (even though some of the best learning comes through painful changes, I think). Do the old scissors trick. Take a printed version of your paper and arbitrarily cut out paragraphs. Shuffle the mess like a deck of cards, throw it up in the air, let a cool breeze float through the pieces—anything to lose the original order. Then, without looking, reassemble them. Don't cheat and try to match up the jagged edges. See what you have—see what kinds of new connections you can make. If you hate it, then by all means go back to the original. You might be surprised with what you find, however; my students almost always are.

Even if you don't get a wildly exciting paper out of this rearrangement exercise, at least it should help show you the ways in which people perceive hypertext writing to be chaotic and random.

After all, remember the newspaper analogy. What in your paper do you prize? What do you want your readers to know or see or understand above all? Think of this as front-page business. What information do you present that relies upon fundamental concepts that you've expressed earlier in your paper? How will you arrange the navigation menu or anchors in order to encourage your reader to follow the order you suggest? Or, do you want go wild and create an experimental piece that can be read in any order?

I think that it's obvious by now that there are many, many different ways to go about assembling a print paper into a hypertext creation—but think of the freedom (the freedom!) that there is. Hypertext puts you firmly in control. You're the newspaper editor. How will you arrange your copy?

Fluidity

Ahh, fluidity: an enemy or a friend? Once you have made decisions about the new order of your paper (assuming that you have chopped the paper to death and have wildly rearranged it—otherwise, skip this part and move on to the next subheading), how do you reassemble a meaningful piece of writing?

Realize that, like it or not, we live in a world of transitions. Papers live in this world, too. If I didn't believe that hypertext weren't valuable, I wouldn't write what I'm about to (nor would I have written this piece at all, frankly): some of the most insightful and meaningful connections that you will come up with in your writing will come from a scissored-up paper that you rearrange. Why? New connections. You force yourself to mesh and meld and melt your ideas together. You're synthesizing and analyzing. This is writing.

And so, for fluidity, I have relatively little to say to you except that you'll need new transitions when you hypertextualize a paper. Consider the visual breaks that you'll leave in the paper when you transition. What do you do with the space that's left (besides create a new transition)?

Citations and Bibliography Work

If hypertext revision was made for anything, this is it. If your paper uses them, the bibliography and in-text citations are the natural teammates of hyperlinks. And, with the increasing use of databases and websites as sources, the hyperlink makes sense.

Paul wrote several papers about his enthusiasm for everything dealing with cars and motors. He used a ton of sources, and he quoted from them within his paper frequently. In the parentheses where the citation would normally go (Szczepanski 2004, 1), Paul inserted the standard text and linked it to his bibliography page at the end of the document. (This might be selfish, but as a teacher who checks sources, I think this is a fantastic time-saver.)

Using a navigation menu, Paul even split his last paper down into four separate parts: first draft, second draft, last draft, and annotated bibliography. And, within the annotated bibliography, every website cited included a hyperlink leading back to that site.

Beyond this sort of hyperlinking being easy for the teacher, it's easy for you, too: you know where your sources are, how you get to them, and how you point others to them, too.

Navigation Menus and Tables of Contents

You may rightly think that a paper you write is insufficiently long and couldn't nearly require a table of contents. I might agree. But, when you look at the table of contents as a navigation menu, more possibilities emerge.

One student, Chris, wrote a paper in which he chose to use different voices to address his views on religion. He took the stances of a Christian talking about Islam and a Buddhist talking about Judaism (among others). Since he was familiar with most of the fundamental concepts of these religions, he was able to weave together a coherent, insightful paper about his relationship with spirituality using a variety of different voices; however, the presence of many voices can be confusing to a reader. Chris' first draft used a long narrative that was hard to follow, and it was mainly him addressing different religions with his own voice. By integrating a sidebar menu, he was able to split the paper into several sections. In fact, the idea to use different voices occurred to him only *after* he saw the possibilities of a navigation menu. For those of us who cannot for the life of us figure out what *else* to do to one of our papers, the conversion to hypertext often leads to innovative and inspirational ideas.

What I find even more interesting about this approach is that Chris realized that his paper functioned well as a nonlinear representation of writing: the reader could bounce back and forth nearly at random between Chris' musings and still fully comprehend the message he was trying to get across.

As if this story alone weren't enough, consider this: I ask my students to assemble a portfolio of their semester's entire work into one easy-to-manage website. In this instance, a navigation menu is a must. How else would I find whatever it is that I'm looking for? And, the writer has the added benefit of being able to keep track for himself where on the site he posted his papers— he doesn't continually have to remember the URL address of each individual page. A simple click, and there he is.

Hyperlinks: Use Them

Another of the papers that I asked my students to write was one in which they explained, to a layperson, how a specific piece of technology works. John chose to explain to his audience the way Flash—the animated sort of stuff you see on some webpages when you first log on to them—works in webpages. Within the text, he integrated hyperlinks from other websites and corporations that demonstrate a sophisticated and not so sophisticated use of Flash. With tree-based media, there's no way that John would be able to show the jumping around and animated nature of a Flash introduction. His paper was enhanced greatly by his ability to demonstrate to his audience visually what exactly it was that he was writing about. He even used a Flash introduction to his own site.

Others of my students have integrated relevant hyperlinks into their documents. I once had a group of students write a webzine about the history of Wal-Mart. Naturally, including hyperlinks to Wal-Mart's site was apropos. The group also included links to sites that bash Wal-Mart as a consumer's power-hungry nightmare as well as to Wal-Mart fan sites (they exist; I've seen them).

What's great about hyperlinking is that it allows readers to continue their own education. Your paper could very well be the inspiration for your readers to enhance their own learning and reading of a subject. Or not. Remember: it's all about options.

Pictures, Photography, Other Media

Are visual media appropriate for a hypertext document? Don't let the *text* in *hypertext* fool you. Text is only one of an astounding number of media options available. Let's say that you're writing a paper on the way jets circulate air within the passenger cabin. In your original paper, you painstakingly explain the way in which a turbine engine sucks in air, heats it, then releases it to the ventilation system aboard a Boeing 777. You spend paragraph after paragraph explaining what mechanisms do what. In your hypertext version, why not use a picture, or, better yet, an animated GIF file or small video file to illustrate what you're talking about?

Of course, detail is always welcome in your paper—but balance is also an essential element when you write. Why spend pages upon pages explaining how a concept or idea works when a picture will allow you to show, in a shorter space, what it is that you're talking about? And, doing this also frees up space in your paper for you to address other topics that are especially relevant.

And think about this, too: a paper you write on music might very well be enhanced with a scholarly little clip of the songs you reference; artworks you discuss might tell more on their own if you show them; the movie trailer of the film you're reviewing might add depth to your analysis—in short, integrating media helps.

On the other hand, you do have to be concerned about copyright infringement. The court is (literally) still out on this one, so here's the advice I give to my students: The Internet, though intended for military use, is now a common tool that untold numbers access daily. We use it to *share* information, and people (not private organizations) are often happy to spread the wealth. When you find an image that you want to include in your paper, it's always polite to email the webmaster of the site to obtain permission. Nine times out of ten, if the use you have for the picture is academic, the author has no problem. If you never get a response, and the picture is *not* marked with the copyright symbol (©), go ahead and use it. If it *is* marked with the ©, and you don't get a response, unfortunately, the image isn't yours for the taking. Remember: you should at all times indicate the URL from which you've obtained the picture, and if you've made the image, give yourself the credit, too.

Other Material

Let's take Trevor, for instance. I asked my students to write a paper in which they interviewed a friend or roommate about his or her computer and Internet habits. Trevor did so, and when he converted his paper to the Web, he also added the transcription of the interview (which he conducted through IM). Rather than placing the interview before or after the actual text of his essay, he hyperlinked it to the front. By doing this, Trevor is allowing the reader to make a choice: Do I read the interview or not? And there are, of course, different reasons a person might want to read the interview: perhaps the integrated quotes within Trevor's paper are funny. Or, maybe Trevor didn't thoroughly explore a topic that the reader found particularly interesting, and the reader hopes that he can find more information within the text of the interview.

Trevor's was a novel idea. He augmented the scope of (and commitment to) his paper by adding a simple, optional piece of text.

So Ends the Benefits: What to Watch Out For

A hypertext paper can explode in size and scope and lose its focus quickly if you let it. Aside from other writing problems that you'll encounter, I find only a few to be hypertext-specific (I don't count being blocked, poor topic choices, etc.), and they are (1) the incredible explosion of material that you'll be tempted to add to your paper, (2) the sometimes time-consuming process of making a hypertext document, (3) the temptation to spend way, way, way too much time on a hypertext paper, and (4) losing your work to an unknown act of your computer.

With anything new, we tend to get excited. We throw in more graphics than we need, or we add video and sound clips that are only tangentially related to the aim of the assignment. Every time you're tempted to add a multimedia object to your work, or you're tempted to insert a hyperlink, hold your fingers and count to ten. Wait. Ride this one out, my friend. Ask yourself if you need it. Maybe more important, ask yourself, Why did I want it in the first place?

As for time consumption, it might be rough going the first time you make a webpage, but it gets easier with the more practice you have. And think about it this way: webpage building is a skill that many employers now look for, and with the world increasingly Internet-dominated, you really can't afford to remain ignorantly in the shadows for much longer.

My third concern goes hand in hand with my first one: the more possibilities you see, the more tempted you'll be to spend much more time on the project than you would a normal paper. While I always advocate spending more time working on your writing, it's the focus on the nontext elements that might land you in hot water. You don't want to spend all night playing with Flash and images just so you can bang out a few pages of text in ten minutes right before class starts. Pace yourself and keep it in perspective.

Computers freeze up sometimes. It's happened to me, it's happened to you, it will continue to happen to the world. There's no fix for this. Save, and save often. If you're working on something terribly important, and you don't want to lose all of your information, place an egg timer next to your computer and set it to go off every five or ten minutes (or longer) to remind you to click the "save" button. The extra time it takes to get the timer and twist it could save you hours upon hours of work.

Go Forth

If you're reading this, chances are that your instructor is incorporating hypertext into his or her classroom. So much the better for you. If you've mysteriously appeared here (also good for you), and what I've talked about sounds appealing, approach your instructor and ask for permission to write hypertext. More often than not, he or she will agree. After all, instructors like new and different too.

Be cutting edge. Be new. Understand that revision begins at home; after that, all bets are off. I sometimes hear students in the hallways complaining that their writing courses are no fun (one girl bemoaned that she wanted to gouge her eyes out with a blunted pencil—I promise this is true). Here's an axiom that's served me well: You're only going to get out of your writing what you put into it. Next time you're asked to revise, for this or some other class, ask yourself "Why not hypertext?" It'll work. It always does.

Reprise

Before You Begin, Ask Yourself: Questions for Revising Hypertext

Arrangement

1. Do I want my reader to be able to read linearly?
   - If yes, cut and paste the paper. Stop.
   - If no, read on.
2. Do I want my reader to have to navigate for herself? If yes, see "Navigation" below. If no, ask:

- If I hide the navigation menu, what happens?
- If I add links at the bottom of the page (or within it), where do they go and why?
- At what points in my paper do I slice and dice the text in order to make separate pieces?

3. Where will my bibliography go? End? Beginning? Throughout?

Navigation

1. Will I add a navigation menu, or will I construct the paper linearly (i.e., give the reader no choice but to continually move forward)?
   - If you will add a menu, read on.
   - If you won't add a menu, cut and paste and hyperlink to the next page at the bottom.

2. If I add the navigation menu, will it appear on every page?
   - Will it be the same for every page?
   - Will it differ?
   - When might it be appropriate for the menu to be different?
   - Will my new pages load in the same window once someone clicks a menu item?
   - What are the advantages and disadvantages of loading new pages in the same window?

3. Am I at peace with the idea of letting my reader *not* read everything I've written?
   - If yes, then hyperlink away.
   - If no, then think about ways you can structure the menu so that you can naturally and subconsciously lure the reader to the parts of your paper and work that you most want him to see.

Hyperlinking

1. Primarily, what will I use hyperlinks for?
   - Links within my own paper to other parts of it (these are called *relative links*)?
   - Links to the bibliography?
   - Links within the same page (these are called *anchors*)?

2. If I'm linking to other parts of my paper, in what areas would hyperlinks naturally occur? If I'm writing linearly, are these even relevant?

3. If I'm linking to other sites, am I doing it just to do it, or will doing so really add something to my paper?

Images

1. What will I gain by adding images?
2. Am I adding them just because?

3. What will the inclusion of a graph do for a paper about Irish setters?

4. What will the inclusion of a photo do for a paper about economics?

5. Where do I place images? Within the text? Beside it? On another page?

6. Are there copyright issues involved? Whom do I contact for permission (usually the website owner)?

Other Media

1. What kinds of other media do I want in my paper?
   - Sound files?
   - Movie files?
   - Flash and animation?

2. What's the added benefit of adding media?
   - Am I adding it to get out of writing? To take up space?
   - Or am I adding it because if the reader sees it, she will have a deeper, broader understanding of what I'm aiming for?

3. How big are the files?
   - Big files aren't efficient for dialup users.
   - Small files are of low quality and might obscure exactly what it is you want to show in the first place.

After Words

Thank You, Thank You Very Much: Coauthors On Collaborative Revision

Hans Ostrom and Wendy Bishop
Wendy Bishop and Hans Ostrom

Wendy—Having been in graduate school together, eons ago, we remet accidentally at a conference twelve years later and found we'd been doing the same sorts of things—teaching writing and creative writing and asking questions about writing practices. I know it was your suggestion, Hans, "Let's do something together," that got us started. In fact, you'll often say that, just that: "Let's do something together," and we start another project.

It was comfort, and a familiarity with each others' background that helped make coauthoring possible (and led to lot's of corevising). I think the very act of talking about almost any subject strikes such a cord of wacky congruence that we both want to (a) write, and, (b) write together as a form of extended talk and sharing. That suggests collaborators might look for—if not common beliefs—at least a common sense of humor and a willingness to listen, each to the other. Coauthors should take pleasure in the other's approach to world and thought.

Because *co*-authoring proved fun, it became easy for me to say back to you: "What should we do next?"

We began by exchanging and then coauthoring poems and then a conference paper. We've done so much—writing to and fro since then—aided by the seemingly miraculous and timely invention of email—that now I can't quite remember a time we didn't write together.

Hans—Besides this shared *vision* (too pretentious a word), we have a laconic effect, I'd say a Why Not? attitude toward projects, authorship, and so forth. I'm not exactly sure why, but from the first we seemed to set egos aside or, more accurately maybe, just always find ways to mesh egos. We've found the collaborative writing pleasurable, too. I feel that, when I collaborate with you, I will often write something different or better or both than I would have on my own. There's an enormous sense of possibility—regardless of the genre into which we are about to travel.

Wendy—Different and better yes. There are times when I've found myself drafting toward or into something you've shared and thought: "How does he know that? What a smart man. He made me understand it perfectly." So appreciating the sensibility of a coauthor is important and enjoying where that mind takes you. I could count on you to be (1) well read, (2) unafraid of what you had read; that is, looking at it for what was useful to you, and (3) humorous but cogent.

Your ability to read and assimilate and connect ideas should seem dazzling, but I've simply come to expect it. We're both the sort who likes to move ahead. We do a lot of egging on, one of the other—send teasing (OK, nagging) emails to be sure work is on-going. We light the candle of one project when our candle is only midway burned down because we're pretty certain that, once rolled into motion, we'll continue and soon need a new project. I don't think any of this is conscious. We're like a team of oxen who once yoked and finding we can pull together, lean forward into the job. "That field plowed? Fine. Where's the next field?"

Hans—Probably an observer would say you and I converse surprisingly little. We both have private personae rather different from our public personae, don't we? Meaning we're relatively reserved, laid-back, and laconic in day-to-day conversations even if we've developed more performance-oriented (too strong a term) personae for our work (teaching writing). Like most longtime colleagues, we have a shorthand code-talk—yes? I remember so many conversations about a project where it's "mumble, mumble, mumble" and then "OK, then, let's do that," and we've sorted out a fairly major wrinkle, problem, task. We hardly ever argue or debate when we disagree because who cares who wins? We used to use letters to iron out details of projects, but now email is just splendid. It's fast and conversational, and we can preserve much of the shorthand and *code*. The one difference I've noted with email is that if one person is in a rotten mood it's a little harder to read the mood than if we were sharing coffee and talking face to face.

Wendy—We did realize early in our work together on that we have similar moods—we're both cup-half-fullers in a way that makes us, oddly, a full 8 ounce when we combine forces. Our process expectations are low so we're always pleased to get anywhere in our writing or cowriting.

After we wax ironic and sarcastic in response to criticism or challenging encouragement, revising becomes less problematic and we say, "To hell with that reviewer, let's just do it."

Hans—We figure we have nothing much to lose in the ego-stakes (but that should never ever be confused with having no ego).

Wendy—There is nothing more luminous than a product. That is, a product in the past, which we now mostly ignore. We're write-aholics, eager to get going again. We thrive on breaking rules, doing what we're told we shouldn't do, exceeding expectations.

Hans—I'd say we're both *finishers*. We don't mind drafting, revising, cogitating, but there's always that goal of finishing. Personally, I've never liked writers who just WON'T finish projects. Maybe it's my working-class background. I think you are probably a more extensive reviser than I am. What do you think?

Wendy—I hadn't thought of this finishing as a class issue but I can see that (still, don't forget I grew up Army-kid-class). For me it's a thought issue too. Since I learn by having written and I love to learn, I tend to keep revising in order to discover smaller learnings. For me, these add up to bigger learnings. Can I learn from others: journals, friends, writers, thinkers? Of course, do and can and will. But there's something about corevising, about your vocabulary that is very good for my writing. It involves an immense amount of wordplay at the sentence level and an avoidance of jargon. In a way, you give me permission to play. I'm thinking here of the introduction to an edited collection of essays that you drafted first. Unworried, you just jumped in. Then you passed the draft to me and so it goes.

   We've learned to recognize and trust our revising patterns and learn from the other's. You're a terrific outliner. And I think I'm getting better at preorganizing from observing this. When I get bogged in working an idea out at the paragraph/section level, you scan the entire text, take out a pen and re-outline a project.

   I see you as being more radical in drafts. I'm sometimes the clean-up crew or the one who says, "Well we could but we probably shouldn't do that." Although we're both sloppy at the beginning, finding form through thinking aloud on paper in our early drafts, you're sloppy because you're a fewer drafts person (then on to the next project). I'm sloppy because I gnaw bigger patches of text to death with small-scale revisions—changing a word, rebalancing sentence shape, treating a paragraph like a poem. Because of this, if I get too exhausted to edit well, you can charge back into the drafts and find my *typos* and simple errors like a clerk, 'tsking at the mess I've made. This isn't to say you like doing this. You're just able at that point in our joint process to do this.

Hans—Obviously, we'd both prefer to be copy edited by a really fine copy editor (like any authors we've sometimes had less than fine ones). We're hard to edit though because we both push our style a lot, try to write in alternate styles. I'd say our alternate style—the way we read each other's drafts may actually *be* the way we talk to each other.

Wendy—Yes, drafting dialogue. That's why I feel OK dismantling some of your more outrageous play or translating it into something a little less facetious. If you don't like that, you'd talk (write) it back in.

Hans—We don't just correct or change the other, though. If I remember correctly, we just up-front give each other permission to *write over* each other's drafts. With some of our work—much of our work—I quite literally forget who wrote what sometimes, even if I am so-called *lead* editor. I read the draft so many times and that contributes to the blurring. But I can't explain fully why we're so comparatively ego-less when we collaborate—especially when in other spheres we have *plenty ego*! I guess there's this sense that it's the work that counts—we're producing something, so *whatever works, works.*

Wendy—Early on I realized we were comfortably *writing over* the other. I always ask other collaborators if they mind my doing this and would they please do it to my return drafts, but it takes them some time to believe I won't get mad if they change *my* words. How can they be *my* words when we're thinking in writing together?

Hans—In practice, we know writing and revising are fluid processes, but the professional worlds of *creative* and *literary* writing (but not of scientific writing) say writers should write alone.

Wendy—We don't seem to care who begins or whose name is down as first author. We may alternate first author if the other person initiated the first draft. But the second author to touch the draft is always free to write over the first and sometimes ends up doing the majority of the work on that project.

Hans—And the initiating author is free to reverse that write-over. Endless. Of course we've internalized each other's habits—sentence to thought to organization—to the degree that I can write "Wendy-only" prose: mostly, but not completely.

Wendy—I'd say in every text I write there's now at least one move that I could point to as a definite "Hans-influence"—could I edit that out? Sure. Would I? Rarely. Ideas don't seem precious either—sometimes one of us comes up with a cool idea the other might envy. Sometimes I decide to myself that it would be better or more useful to write a thing myself or with other authors (I may be trying to mentor a grad student or want to try to co-compose with others for the change); the same is true for Hans. We don't present ourselves as always writing together. But I think we find comfort and harmony in having that as a background (that sometimes moves to foreground) for our writing lives. When we're emailing drafts, it's about that common passion, writing. Demonstrably, we've done some of our best thinking, writing, revising together. Does it matter so much if you change my phrase when you improve my punctuation? No, both improve a sentence that is going to be attributed to us both. And while we like revision, who doesn't wish it were easier sometimes? With a coreviser, it actually is.

Hans—In one co-project, we each contributed different writing exercises. The editors asked us to sign our initials to, then not to sign, then to sign initials to the individual exercises and at the end of those transitions from *I* to *we* to *I* again, this *writing over* process became more clear. Eventually, I could only tell who wrote what if individual family stories signaled a historical or factual *I*.

Wendy—And it goes beyond influence to resource. I can now *assign myself to write like Hans* in order to get out of a drafting problem spot, and that's wonderfully freeing. I can import what I imagine to be your *to hell with the audience* approach and break through some useless propriety that is holding me back from trying out ideas in a draft.

I'd be interested to know if you see me as more pragmatic as I sometimes see myself and if you ever adopt any of my moves as intentional solutions? What I mean is, does our writing together change the way you write alone?

Hans—In terms of process, I doubt if we've changed each other all that much— I'm talking about the basic day-to-day habits of a writer. What's interesting to me is that the personal habits have little if any negative effect on our collaborations. The influence for me comes when I write poems or criticism or scholarly things alone—I know darn well I've picked up perspectives via osmosis from you—ideas, habits of experimentation, rhetorical moves. Also, it's interesting that with a couple of books you've edited solo, you seem to feel free to just email and say, "Hans, I need this niche filled," and I write an essay to fill it—an essay I probably wouldn't have written if you hadn't asked.

Wendy—Yes, we pinch-hit. I know I can ask you without insult to help out at any time and, even more important, to take an *assignment* (luckily we both like them). Even within the constraints, you manage to create something I wouldn't have expected. Well, I guess I do *expect* the unexpected from you. Meanwhile, I know you are writing substantial scholarly books alone, that you have this perspective and learning as a Langston Hughes scholar, that I couldn't touch. Respect helps maintain the ego balance and let's us listen to each other.

Hans—A few times we've fussed and fumed, but my heart's never in it, and usually we're actually mad at a third party, like an editor or an editorial board, or some third party that just can't *get* what we're doing in our writing. We've known each other for so long that politics—like gender politics—just don't seem to enter into our processes in any huge way. I'm sure I've acted very *male* at times—but it's certainly nothing you can't handle! There is so much creative pleasure most of the time that any creative *tension* is just a road sign on the journey. I sound to myself as if I'm gushing. I don't mean to. I'm as surprised as the next person that we—that any two professionals—have worked together so well so long on such a variety of projects.

Wendy—I'm just as surprised that so few authors try collaborative writing projects. I can't think of a memorable instance of disagreement but plenty when we fueled each others fuming at a writing roadblock (deadline, editor, formatting limit), or the like. Our disagreements happen earlier—as we try out project ideas on each other.

Hans—Yes, the work is the thing when we work together. It probably helps that we have substantial "solo careers." That is, I wonder about people who collaborate so much that they start to get nervous about *authority* and then insecurity builds and things fall apart. A Lennon/McCartney deal. But mainly I like watching how you improve my writing when you change it. Writers like seeing writing made better. I look forward to the day when humanities types don't see collaboration as such a big deal—scientists and social scientists reached that point long ago. I feel as if you and I and a few others were early to the collaborative party and have enjoyed the goodies.

Process Coda—Wendy was sent the request by some writing teacher friends to write about Hans' and her own coauthoring practices. She forwarded the request to Hans and said she'd only do it if he agreed. Hans agreed because he thought it would be a good excuse to think about writing together—to get in work gear and work up a project. Because he said yes, Wendy said yes too. Both of us were already overly committed to solo writing projects, but as soon as the interview became a collaborative venture it became interesting.

The initial self-interview took place in three email exchanges (if phone interviews had been a requirement, it wouldn't have happened at all): Wendy wrote answers to several questions posed by the teachers between classes and ran out of time. Hans answered and continued (ditto the out of time). Wendy wrote back and extended. Clean up. Reread. Learn. If it had taken more than that, we'd not have done it. To do it with less than all our energies, though, would have been impossibly unlike us.

We looked forward to reading each other, to the returned text. One last reread reminded us to add that contrary to what it sounds like, we do value other things: families, gardening, teaching writing, videos, reading, traveling, and eating are some of those things (and writing poetry *because it is there*). But, there isn't a time, either, when learning about writing can't arrest us in midtracks, preoccupy our minds all day, all night until, there, we have to say and see what we've said. At the end of this interview warm-up, we started exchanging emails about the next project, a coedited collection on writers and storytelling.

Two years later, we have just returned to our email interview and revised it. Meanwhile, *The Subject Is Story*, which we coedited, is in print and we're on to other collaborative work.

So thank you dear readers, thank you very much.

We leave it to you to decide if just one of us or both of us (or neither of us) wrote this last word.

About the Authors

Wendy Bishop was fascinated by sentences and by any options that allowed writers to experiment with style—issues that are highlighted in edited and coedited collections like *Elements of Alternate Style* and *Genre and Writing*, published by Heinemann. She and Hans Ostrom worked to convince literary journal editors to value poetry as much as prose, and at different times in recent years, she'd joined Laura Newton and Devan Cook in writing groups, communal afternoons that allowed them to better understand and value revision.

Devan Cook often revises with the method she was taught in high school by the great Helen Hollander: Throw it out, and start over. Her ideas about revision were also strongly influenced by her father, who asked, "What does *that* mean?" She finds sentences as roomy as suburban houses and their appointments and architecture even more interesting. For further reading and more sentence-level exercises, she recommends Gary and Glynis Hoffman's *Adios, Strunk and White*.

Brock Dethier suggests more ways to use music to learn about revision in his book *From Dylan to Donne: Bridging English and Music*. His descriptive outline first appeared in *The Composition Instructor's Survival Guide*. Both books are from Heinemann. He teaches writing at Utah State University and wishes to thank the members of his revision group, FHE, for their help.

Maggie Gerrity is an essayist, poet, and writer of fiction, as well as a teacher of writing. She is an avid fan of alternate style and encourages her students to employ the same revision methods she uses herself, especially fat drafts, writing between the lines, and always, *always* reading drafts aloud. She received her M.A. from Florida State University and is pursuing a Ph.D. at SUNY Binghamton University.

Because **Melissa A. Goldthwaite** sees writing and revision as inseparable acts, she teaches revision in all of her classes—from creative writing workshops to courses in composition and literature—at Saint Joseph's University. Her most recent major writing-revision project was *The St. Martin's Guide to Teaching Writing*, published in 2003.

Alice S. Horning's favorite research project is the one reported in her recent book, *Revision Revisited*. By watching experienced professional writers work on revising, she was able to observe the processes by which good writing is produced. It was a fascinating experience. Currently, she is continuing research on revision and assembling, with colleagues, a volume in the Electronic Guides to Composition Studies focused on revision and revision processes. In addition, she has begun a new book on the historical development of literacy and its implications for the psycholinguistic processes of reading and writing in the digital age.

Dana Kantrowitz believes if we further examine our own and other writers' revision processes we will not only grow as writers and teachers of writing but will find we are as varied in our styles, voices, and characters as we are in our methods of putting them onto paper. She is currently pursuing her M.A. in poetry at Florida State University and is teaching composition for the first time.

Laura Newton is a poet and writing teacher who believes revision is fun and challenging. Sometimes she enjoys revision more than writing the original draft. Her favorite method of revision is memory drafting, writing the draft from memory of the previous draft without looking at the text, because it allows for surprise in the revision process. Currently she is revising the poems in her dissertation for a Ph.D. in Creative Writing at Florida State University.

Hans Ostrom likes to write the first draft of a poem on the right-hand page of a notebook so that the left-hand page is immediately available for revision work. A recent chapbook of his poems is *Subjects Apprehended*, and he's also published *A Langston Hughes Encyclopedia*, along with several books cowritten with Wendy Bishop, with whom he's been revising poetry and prose since the mid-1970s in Central California.

Jay Szczepanski is a strong believer in multimedia methods of composition, including, but certainly not limited to, hypertext and Web-based writing. He follows the advice of Andrew Dillon, one of his favorite poets: You don't have a poem unless you have a stack of drafts a foot tall on your kitchen floor. Jay thinks that the same holds true for hypertext, its newness and technology notwithstanding.

Further Reading

Anderson, Daniel, and Bret Benjamin, Christopher Busiel, and Bill Paredes-Holt. 1998. *Teaching Online: Internet Research, Conversation and Composition.* 2d ed. New York: Longman.

Baron, Naomi S. 2000. Alphabet to Email: How Written English Evolved and Where It's Heading. New York: Routledge.

Bishop, Wendy, ed. 1997. *Elements of Alternate Style: Essays on Writing and Revision.* Portsmouth, NH: Boynton/Cook.

Bizzell, Patricia, and Helen Fox, eds. 2002. *AltDis: Alternative Discourses and the Academy.* Portsmouth, NH: Boynton/Cook.

Bolker, Joan. 1986. *Writing Your Dissertation in Fifteen Minutes a Day: A Guide to Starting, Revising, and Finishing Your Doctoral Thesis.* Indianapolis, IN: John Wiley and Sons.

Bridwell-Bowles, Lillian. 1992. "Discourse and Diversity: Experimental Writing within the Academy." *College Composition and Communication* 43 (3): 349–68.

———. 1995. "Freedom, Form, Function: Varieties of Academic Discourse." *College Composition and Communication* 46 (1): 46–61.

Burroway, Janet. 2002. *Writing Fiction.* 6th ed. New York: Longman.

Clark, James L., and Lyn R. Clark. 2000. *Cyberstyle! The Writer's Complete Desk Reference.* Independence, KY: South-Western College Publishing.

Corbett, Edward P. J., and Robert J. Connors. 1999. *Classical Rhetoric for the Modern Student.* New York: Oxford University Press.

Davis, Robert, and Mark Shadle. 2000. "'Building a Mystery': Alternative Research Writing and the Academic Art of Seeking." *College Composition and Communication* (51) 3: 417–46.

Dillard, Annie. 1989. *The Writing Life.* New York: Harper Perennial.

DiTiberio, John, and George Jensen. 1995. *Writing and Personality: Finding Your Voice, Your Style, Your Way.* Palo Alto, CA: Davies-Black.

Elbow, Peter. 1998. *Writing Without Teachers.* 2d. ed. New York: Oxford University Press.

Fulwiler, Toby. 1999. "A Lesson in Revision." *The Subject Is Writing: Essays by Students and Teachers.* 3d ed., ed. Wendy Bishop, 84–89. Portsmouth, NH: Boynton/Cook.

Goldberg, Natalie. 1986. *Writing Down the Bones.* Boston: Shambhala.

———. 1990. *Wild Mind.* New York: Bantam.

Harris, Robert A. 2003. *Writing with Clarity and Style: A Guide to Rhetorical Devices for Contemporary Writers*. Los Angeles: Pyrczak.

Heard, Georgia. 2002. *The Revision Toolbox: Teaching Techniques That Work*. Portsmouth, NH: Heinemann.

Hoffman, Gary, and Glynis Hoffman. 1999. *Adios, Strunk and White: A Handbook for the New Academic Essay*. 2d ed. Huntington Beach, CA: Verve.

Horning, Alice S. 2002. *Revision Revisited*. Cresskill, NJ: Hampton.

Laib, Nevin K. 1993. *Rhetoric and Style: Strategies for Advanced Writers*. Englewood Cliffs, NJ: Prentice Hall.

Lamott, Anne. 1994. *Bird by Bird: Some Instructions on Writing and Life*. New York: Pantheon.

Lanham, Richard A. 1999a. *Revising Business Prose*. 4th ed. New York: Allyn and Bacon.

———. 1999b. *Revising Prose*. 4th ed. New York: Allyn and Bacon.

Leland, Christopher T. 2002. *Creative Writer's Style Guide: Rules and Advice for Writing Fiction and Creative Nonfiction*. Cincinatti, OH: Story.

Lerner, Betsy. 2000. *The Forest for the Trees: An Editor's Advice to Writers*. New York: Riverhead.

Maddon, David. 1995. *Revising Fiction: A Handbook for Writers*. New York: New American Library.

Murray, Donald. 2004. *The Craft of Revision*. 5th ed. Boston: Heinle.

Quinn, Arthur. 1993. *Figures of Speech: Sixty Ways to Turn a Phrase*. Davis, CA: Hermagoras.

Spooner, Michael. 1997. "Sympathy for the Devil: Editing Alternate Style." In *Elements of Alternate Style: Essays on Writing and Revision*, ed. Wendy Bishop, 149–59. Portsmouth, NH: Boynton/Cook.

Strunk, William, and E. B. White. 2000. *The Elements of Style*. 4th ed. New York: Allyn and Bacon.

Weathers, Winston. 1980. *An Alternate Style: Options in Composition*. Portsmouth, NH: Boynton/Cook. (Out of print; check your library.)

———. 1990. "The Grammars of Style: New Options in Composition." In *Rhetoric and Composition: A Sourcebook for Teachers and Writers*, 3d ed., ed. Richard L. Graves, 200–14. Portsmouth, NH: Boynton/Cook.

Williams, Joseph M. 2002. *Style: Ten Lessons in Clarity and Grace*. 7th ed. New York: Longman.

Willis, Meredith Sue. 1993. *Deep Revision*. New York: Teachers and Writers.

AEJ-2145